DEAR
JOHNNY
DEERE

PRAIRIE PLAY SERIES NO. 32

Dear Johnny Deere

A PLAY BY
KEN CAMERON

BASED ON THE MUSIC AND LYRICS OF
FRED EAGLESMITH

NeWest Press

Library and Archives Canada Cataloguing in Publication

Cameron, Ken, 1969–, author
Dear Johnny Deere / Ken Cameron.

(Prairie play series ; 32) ISBN 978-1-927063-82-8 (pbk.)

I. Title.
II. Series: Prairie play series ; 32

PS8605.A482D43 2015   C812'.6   C2014-906471-3

Editor: Anne Nothof
Book design: Natalie Olsen, Kisscut Design
Author photo: Bryce Meyer
Production photos: Terry Manzo

For professional or amateur production rights, please contact:
Michael Petrasek, The Talent House
204A St. George Street
Toronto, Ontario M5R 2N5
416-960-9686
michael@talenthouse.ca

NeWest Press acknowledges the support of the Canada Council for the Arts, the Alberta Foundation for the Arts, and the Edmonton Arts Council for support of our publishing program. We acknowledge the financial support of the Government of Canada through the Canada Book Fund for our publishing activities.

201, 8540 – 109 Street
Edmonton, Alberta T6G 1E6
780.432.9427
NeWest Press   www.newestpress.com

No bison were harmed in the making of this book.

Printed and bound in Canada

For Rita, who encouraged me to do the work required
for a full emotional life;

for my parents who first showed me love of the land,
for my grandfather who showed me how to love a tractor

and for Fred, who sang about these things.

CONTENTS

Dear Johnny Deere

FOREWORD BY THE COMPOSER

I lived this play — from my early childhood to my late teens when I basically hitchhiked off the farm and into pop culture. So it is interesting for me to look at this former existence of mine. Much like an old high school jacket. When I take it out of the closet, I think of all the things I could've said which might have made that jacket so much cooler. At the end of the day, though, I feel like Ken has captured an essence of what was going on at that time in my life. There are parts that he has magnified that maybe I wouldn't have. And conversely, he has diminished things I wouldn't have.

Some of the chords to the songs are wrong — as they should be. Some of the facts are wrong — as they should be.

This isn't a literal representation.

I initially thought that writing a foreword to a book about my life is a little egotistical. On top of that, I haven't been a huge fan of live theatre for a long time, and that is why I did not want to write the foreword to this book. But Ken Cameron, in his reasonable yet badgering fashion (he gets things done), has twisted my arm and here I am.

I am here because this play isn't about me or my work as much as it is about that hardscrabble clay county that we knew as the township of Caistor.

It's about all the people who don't live there anymore. And an entire community that was wiped out by changing times and a less than sympathetic Canadian government. I am actually a lucky one — I'm a successful Canadian artist who gets to drink unreasonable amounts of Spanish wine on summer lawns with the cast of this play as they sit around and talk about me and my work.

It feels like some kind of redemption to me. It feels a bit like justice. It feels like I got the story out — not my story, but our story.

This, of course, is as much as anyone could ask for.

Fred Eaglesmith

INTRODUCTION BY THE DIRECTOR

This story begins with the worst pitch in the history of Canadian playwriting. It begins with a playwright, a bunch of songs, an idea, the Blyth Festival, the Banff Centre for the Arts and the Calgary Tower. It actually begins a bit earlier, but in homage to the unreliable narrator who figures so prominently in the play itself, I'll just leap ahead to what I have already called the worst pitch in the history of Canadian playwriting. To be fair, there was nothing wrong with the pitch itself. I suppose that the real culprit in this story was circumstance. And it goes something like this...

In 2011, I was visiting Calgary for Alberta Theatre Projects' annual playRites Festival, near the end of my ten-year stint as artistic director of the Blyth Festival, southern Ontario's beloved cradle of new Canadian work. Earlier in the year, I had agreed to Ken Cameron's suggestion that the Blyth Festival should commission his new work based on the songs of bad-boy folk icon Fred Eaglesmith. The partnership made eminent sense: Ken's earlier play, *Harvest*, had gone gangbusters in Blyth, and the hardscrabble aesthetic of Eaglesmith's songs seemed like a match made in heaven for our rural audience. But Ken had never worked on a musical before, so we agreed that we would need considerable workshop time before production. Enter the Banff Centre...

Ken called me a few days before I arrived in Calgary and said that he had arranged a meeting with musical theatre genius Kelly Robinson of the Banff Centre, and that he was hoping to broker a deal between Banff and Blyth to share development expenses. His plan was simple: get me and Kelly settled around a comfortable breakfast in Calgary's favorite downtown diner and let the magic of carbohydrates, cowboy ambience and caffeine do the rest. The only hitch, we were to discover a few days later, was that the diner in question had closed.

"No problem," Ken enthused. "We'll have breakfast at the top of the Calgary Tower. It's perfect."

I suggested that this was likely to be quite expensive, but he dismissed my concerns. Oozing his particular brand of confidence, Ken assured me that "they don't charge for the elevator ride if you're going up to eat and the menu is very reasonable."

The revolving restaurant in the Calgary Tower, typical of tourist attractions, was designed with novelty rather than practicality in mind. In this case, the novelty of constant revolution overruled the practical concern of motion sickness. No sooner had the three of us settled at a table, but Kelly and I began to feel dizzy and nauseous, respectively. The arrival of eggs, swathed in hollandaise and bacon, did nothing to ease the nausea. In fact, quite the opposite effect took hold. We nonetheless embarked on a determinedly practical discussion on the nature of musicals — and jukebox musicals in particular. We agreed that the companies could co-develop the piece onsite in Banff the following autumn and that we would find a strong musical dramaturg to join the team. The eggs, alas, sat mostly untouched throughout the meeting. I gamely tried to down my share, but the slow, steady spin of the room, coupled with a merciless sun, forced me to give up. And it was only when the bill arrived that I felt truly sick: breakfast for three came to slightly less than $100.

Despite such an inauspicious beginning, the workshop went ahead and, thanks to all involved, it is firmly entrenched as one of the favourite experiences of my career. For a week we enjoyed the breathtaking scenery and hospitality of the Banff Centre as the play underwent radical surgery at the hands of Ken, musical director David Archibald, musical dramaturg Neil Bartram and myself. Songs were discarded, songs were added, songs were reassigned to different characters, songs were scrutinized for active content... every song was forced to justify its place in the story. Ken provided an endless stream of rewrites to accommodate the radical shift that was underway. We exercised ruthless demands on the material, but the reason that the process moved steadily forward was that Ken signed on to collaborate from the moment we set foot in that studio. There was no ego to get in the way, because he exercised nothing but an objective determination to improve the narrative. Perhaps this was a product of working with someone else's source material, but I believe that it speaks directly to Ken's selfless desire to make good art. It is not about praise or ownership or pride when you work with Ken: it's about making the story move with intent and passion.

I have had the great pleasure of directing several productions of *Dear Johnny Deere* and, as I write this, I look forward to reviving it at Theatre Calgary in the spring of 2015. Like Fred Eaglesmith himself, this play is an unlikely hero: coarse, raw, loud, full of unapologetic cliché and tenderness that masquerades as silence. For me, the greatest pleasure has been working with the tornado that is Ken Cameron. I will be forever grateful that he invited me along for the ride, even if he does still owe me $50 for a breakfast that I could not eat.

Playwright's Retort: I want it on record that after reading the first draft of this introduction, I sent an electronic money transfer to Eric Coates for $50 with the subject line "Here's your blood money." As of publication, it remains uncashed...

Eric Coates

A WORD FROM THE PLAYWRIGHT

In selecting the songs for *Dear Johnny Deere*, I watched Fred perform several times and listened repeatedly to all seventeen albums Fred had at that point recorded. (He has since recorded three more just over the short lifetime of this play.) I made a comprehensive list of each song, its plot and its similarities to other songs in Fred's repertoire. I learned that Fred's songs are populated by small-time crooks, small-town loners, failed farmers, unfaithful women, working-class heroes and unreliable narrators. His between-song banter is both wry and cranky, poorly disguising a generous heart and giving nature. In retrospect, I realize that immersing myself in the songs and live performances meant that I was able to semi-consciously imbue these characteristics into the characters.

In the end I managed to select forty-four songs. As I began to write, I managed to whittle that list down to a mere twenty-four and a plot that involved two brothers, two wives, both parents and a slew of neighbours. Thanks to a workshop with Daniel MacIvor, that character list was narrowed even further and hammered into what is essentially the plotline that you have in your hands. I will forever be indebted to Daniel for suggesting that Caroline never, ever apologize outright for her infidelity and that instead, the couple should find another path to reconciliation. Any performers tackling those parts should be keenly aware of that responsibility.

I also owe a great debt to Kelly Robinson and the Banff Centre for the Arts, who worked with the Blyth Festival to create an intensive developmental workshop with musical dramaturg Neil Bertram. Neil provided me with a crash course in musical theatre structure. I was experienced enough to already be familiar with the basic rule that the character(s) should exit each song in a very different state than they enter it. We chose those of Fred's songs which most read like O. Henry short stories — the ones with a distinctive voice, a clear narrative arc and a twist ending — because we felt they would translate best to the stage.

I may owe the greatest acknowledgement to director Eric Coates, who uncovered the central metaphor of Johnny's musical life: his silence. It's odd to conceive of the lead character in a musical as silent, but Eric determined early on that, as far as Johnny was concerned, talking about feelings was for city folk. Eric managed to convince me that Johnny should say as little as possible until finally he can't help but break into song. Together Eric and I took a red pen to Johnny's lines. Where there were two sentences, we viciously cut one. Whenever we spied a sub-clause, we took it out. If we could get away with it, we had him grunt. The result was the powerful, explosive relationship that actors J.D. and Rebecca brought to life and which had Jeff desperately ducking for cover.

David Archibald's sensitive and clever arrangements for these songs showcase their great range, and he made an extra effort to make each song as distinctive as possible. Fred Eaglesmith's music has been variously labeled "country and western," "folk," "alternative," "alt-country" and "bluegrass." It inspires comparisons to icons as diverse as Woody Guthrie, Bruce Springsteen and Stompin' Tom Connors. But none of these labels really capture the variety that Fred has explored over the thirty-five years of his musical career. Over his twenty-five-year recording career, Fred has managed to both transcend and blend genres and categories.

And finally, none of this would have been possible without Fred himself. When I first approached Fred with this idea, he said, "I think it's a great idea. I'll speak to my agent and you can use any song you want. But I hate theatre. I don't want to be involved in any way. I don't want to see a script and I'll never come to a rehearsal. But you go nuts."

Fred, if you're reading this, I've never properly thanked you for the blank cheque.

Ken Cameron

NOTES ON MUSIC BY THE MUSIC DIRECTOR

Fred Eaglesmith has a singular voice in the world of roots music today. As musical director and arranger, my goal has been to stay true to his musical vision while supporting the dramatic sweep of *Dear Johnny Deere*. It was clear from Ken's earliest draft and Eric's initial vision that the entire cast would be called upon to contribute instrumentally. Fortunately, I was blessed with a fine crew of actor/singer/musicians.

In the premiere production, we employed a rich palette of acoustic instruments: standard and high-string guitars, mandolin, banjo, piano and cajon, as well as electric bass and lap steel to fill out the sound — a lot of wood, a lot of strings, a lot of vibrations. The music wants to be close to the earth.

Fred's hardscrabble upbringing provides the raw material for his music, combining his Canadian farm experience with iconic images from more than thirty-five years of touring the Canadian and American heartland.

Speaking of heartland, what drew me to Fred's songs in the first place was their unique and unyielding sense of heart. The characters may be quirky, the music may not be overly complex, but the stories are strong, and always at their core is an uncommon honesty and truth.

When I listen to his songs, I can almost imagine Fred leaning against a broken-down Blue Bird tour bus trying out some new changes on his guitar while staring across a parched field. It's easy to picture him remembering his own father as he watches an ancient farmer listlessly working a hand-pump at an empty well. It's easy to insert his teenaged hobo self into his pictures of trains and hitchhikers. Fred's rich life and keen eye feed his songs, his love for roots music shapes the sound and the result is a vital contribution to the mythology of rural life.

Anyone wishing to use David's arrangements should contact Michael Petrasek at The Talent House, 204A St. George Street, Toronto, ON, M5R 2N5, (416) 960-9686, michael@ talenthouse.ca.

David Archibald

ACKNOWLEDGEMENTS

Eric Coates, Michael Petrasek, David Archibald, Neil Bartram, Kelly Robinson, Mary Elgersma, Deb Sholdice, Jeff Culbert, Rebecca Auerbach, Jack Nicholsen, Tyler Rive, Esther Purves-Smith, Tony Eyamie, Duval Lang, Lisa Humber, Michael "Spider" Bishop, Cameron MacDuffee, David van Belle, Derek Ritschel, Helen Wagenaar, Alberta Playwrights Network, David Belke, Trevor Reuger, Michelle Kneale, Tracey Carroll, Christopher Hunt, Marshall Hopkins, Doug Curtis, Daniel MacIvor.

Any company producing *Dear Johnny Deere* must reproduce the following Special Thanks in the program:

"*Dear Johnny Deere* was commissioned by the Blyth Festival's Roulston Roy New Play Development Fund and premiered there in June 2012. Its development was supported by a residency at the Banff Centre for the Arts; by financial assistance from the Canada Council for the Arts and the Alberta Foundation for the Arts; with input from the Alberta Playwrights Network; and with a workshop by Lighthouse Theatre in Port Dover, Ontario."

MUSIC PERMISSIONS

"Yellow Barley Straw" — written by Fred Elgersma. © 1999. Critter City Music (SESAC) — administered by Bluewater Music Services Corp. Used by Permission. All Rights Reserved.

"White Trash" — written by Fred Elgersma. © 2001. Critter City Music (SESAC) — administered by Bluewater Music Services Corp. Used by Permission. All Rights Reserved.

"White Rose" — written by Fred Elgersma. © 1996. Critter City Music (SESAC) — Administered by Bluewater Music Services Corp. Used by Permission. All Rights Reserved.

"Spookin' the Horses" — written by Fred Elgersma. © 1998. Critter City Music (SESAC) — Administered by Bluewater Music Services Corp. Used by Permission. All Rights Reserved.

"Small Motors" — written by Fred Elgersma. © 2003. Critter City Music (SESAC) — Administered by Bluewater Music Services Corp. Used by Permission. All Rights Reserved.

"John Deere B" — written by Fred Elgersma. © 2003. Sweetwater Music (SOCAN) — Administered by Bluewater Music Services Corp. Used by Permission. All Rights Reserved.

"I Wanna Buy Your Truck" — written by Fred Elgersma. © 2002. Sweetwater Music (SOCAN) — Administered by Bluewater Music Services Corp. Used by Permission. All Rights Reserved.

"Bench Seat Baby" — written by Fred Elgersma. © 2001. Critter City Music (SESAC) — Administered by Bluewater Music Services Corp. Used by Permission. All Rights Reserved.

"Wilder Than Her" — written by Fred Elgersma. © 1996. Critter City Music (SESAC) — Administered by Bluewater Music Services Corp. Used by Permission. All Rights Reserved.

PRODUCTION HISTORY

Dear Johnny Deere was first produced at the Blyth Festival in Blyth, Ontario in June 2012 with the following cast:

McAllister	Jeff Culbert
Johnny	J.D. Nicholsen
Caroline	Rebecca Auerbach
Mike / Hendrick / Collector	Matthew Campbell
Musician One	David Archibald
Musician Two	Capucine Onn

Director	Eric Coates
Musical Director	David Archibald
Set & Costume Design	Pat Flood
Lighting design	Rebecca Picherack
Stage Manager	Dini Conte
Assistant Stage Manager	Heather Thompson

The play was remounted in 2013 for productions in Blyth and Lighthouse Theatre, Port Dover, with the addition of Jason Chesworth as Mike / Hendrick / Collector, Josephine Ho as Stage Manager, and Rachel Dawn Woods as Assistant Stage Manager.

A second production with important revisions was presented at the Mackenzie Theatre as part of the 2013 Charlottetown Festival with the following cast:

McAllister	Hank Stinson
Johnny	Cameron MacDuffee
Caroline	Amanda LeBlanc
Mike / Hendrick / Collector	Sweeney MacArthur
Musician One	Matthew Campbell
Musician Two	Roy Johnstone
Director	Wade Lynch
Musical Director	Matthew Campbell
Set & Costume Design	Charlotte Dean
Lighting design	Reg "Dutch" Thompson
Stage Manager	Kira Maros

PLAYWRIGHT'S NOTES

This play is a piece of storytelling theatre rather than an attempt at verisimilitude, and its theatricality should therefore be an essential part of its aesthetic. All of the performers will be joining in one another's songs from the side of the stage even if they are not part of the action in a realistic sense.

Therefore the actors should remain onstage and help create the sense that the community is watching the action unfold and that we are all sharing in the telling of this story. Some might sit with the band and play along, if they can make a musical contribution. Others might whittle, or fiddle with a piece of equipment, until it is their turn to take the stage.

In a similar vein, there is no realistic setting, no kitchen with running water, no animals or horses or tractors onstage. There are instead hints of locations, bits and pieces of farm equipment and scenic elements that evoke the audience's imagination rather than complete it.

The most prominent elements of the set are two farmhouses situated one directly beside the other, separated by only a few feet and one whitewashed fence. Other key elements include a hint of an antique John Deere B tractor with its distinctive green hood and large rear wheel; Johnny's Mechanic Shop where he repairs cars and retreats from responsibility; Johnny's mighty big car and its bench seat; and the dirt of the farm that is so much a part of the characters' lives. There are several different spaces off the farm that the script calls for that should be suggested in the set: the liquor store, a neighbouring farm auction, the Royal Canadian Legion Hall, and a local gravel pit where the kids hang out on a Friday night.

SONG LIST

ACT ONE

"Yellow Barley Straw"

"White Trash"

"White Rose"

"Spookin' The Horses"

"Small Motors"

"John Deere B"

"I Wanna Buy Your Truck"

"Bench Seat Baby"

"Wilder Than Her"

"Time To Get A Gun"

ACT TWO

"Yellow Barley Straw" (Reprise)

"Ordinary Guy"

"White Rose" (Reprise)

"Small Motors" (Reprise)

"Old John Deere"

"Freight Train"

"Worked Up Field"

"York Road"

"Wilder Than Her" (Reprise)/Finale

CAST OF CHARACTERS

This is a play for four actors, each of whom must sing.

McAllister, 65, a farmer and publisher of a small-town newspaper
McAllister is jaded and grumpy, the creases in the corners of his eyes worn by years of peering into other people's business. He has seen and reported on it all, from foreclosures to farm accidents, and he is quick to throw up an uncaring façade. He is just as quick to rush to judgment and not shy about telling anyone and everyone he meets exactly why their opinion is wrong. But in truth, he is a softie underneath, and his façade hides an embarrassment at how easily he is moved to care.

Johnny, early 40s, a farmer
Johnny's skin is weathered by years spent planting crops in the heat and splitting wood in the cold; and his face is creased from squinting into the sun looking for rain and from heading out to work in a downpour. If we could see closely, we'd see that Johnny's fingers are always covered in grease, embedded deep in the beds of his fingernails. He's not a man prone to talking about how he feels or why he feels the way he does; he'd rather pick up a heavy implement and do something about what troubles him. If last night he was drunk, there is little trace of it today, other than a husky voice: like many a hard-drinking man, Johnny is rarely hungover, but almost always grumpy in the morning.

Caroline, early 30s, a farmer
Caroline is a good decade younger than Johnny: young enough to have her whole future in front of her, old enough to know that future isn't likely to measure up to what she'd thought it was going to be. There's a restlessness in Caroline's eyes, a wildness that comes not from seeking a good time, but from insisting on living a full life. It's an energy that convinces you she'd be willing to throw it all away

if she felt that's what she needed to do to remain true to what she believed in. And that makes her just as dangerous as Johnny, in her own way. Caroline also voices the Auctioneer.

Hendrik, 50, Johnny's father

Hendrik is a Dutch immigrant to Canada, who has escaped the hardships of post-war Europe to make a new life and find a new family in the promised land. Having lost his wife shortly after she gave birth to Johnny, Hendrik found raising a young boy by himself to be hard and lonely. This loss, coupled with his Calvinist upbringing, has left him severe and stern.

Mike, early 30s, a land speculator

Mike is a former resident of this town who moved to the big city to work for several years in the provincial roads and transportation planning department. Mike was never a popular kid in school, but he has made a success of himself as an adult. His return to the town, to seize upon the real estate deals which he suspects may lie in the wake of the province's plans to build a major highway nearby, is his chance at not only profit, but redemption.

Collector, age indeterminate

The Collector makes a brief appearance in the second act. His eye for a deal and his friendly negotiating skills make for a memorable character turn.

Hendrik, Mike and the Collector are all intended to be played by the same actor.

Dear Johnny Deere

Act one

Johnny sits in his workshop with an unopened envelope in his
hand. Caroline looks at the field taking stock of their life together.
McAllister stands on the opposite side of the fence with his notebook.
Mike stands aloof, waiting to pounce.

MUSIC: "YELLOW BARLEY STRAW"

All (*singing*):   He's got a heart made of Yellow Barley Straw
all wrapped up in calico patches,
and plum-chuck full of love.
He looks out over the fields
every year's losses, every year's yields,
every year's dreams, a hundred bushels
        to an acre...

Johnny takes the unopened envelope and turns it over a few times in his hand.

And tomorrow, y'know,
the bank is gonna come and take it,
        take it all away.
He got a letter in the mail it was only,
why it was only yesterday...

Johnny stands and looks out at the field. He puts the letter away in his pocket,
unopened.

But he just goes on believing...
And you can't sow crops if the ground ain't even.
So he tills the soil, he drills the seed 'til dawn.
His heart is made of yellow barley straw...

The rest of the cast retreats to stools or furniture around the stage or joins
the band if they can make a musical contribution. McAllister stands centre
stage: he will be our Narrator for tonight.

MUSIC: "MCALLISTER'S NARRATOR THEME"

McAllister: That's the thing about farmers, they'll go on believing
even in the face of foreclosure, floods and financial disaster.
They ain't got the business sense God gave a beaver.

The name's McAllister. I run the local. *The Local Paper.* My
father gave it the most imaginative name he could think of at
the time: *The Local Paper.* You can imagine that in the thirty
years since I took it over, I've come up with a pretty long list
of better names. But people in these parts don't like change,
so *The Local Paper.* it has remained.

A light on Johnny and Caroline.

As a newspaperman, it's my job to tell our stories, but you'll
have to help me out a bit. If you're up for it. Though judging
by the looks of you. . . It's all about this here dirt, that there
creek, and a tractor that I'm not about to haul up those stairs
back there. You'll have to imagine the tractor. For that matter,
you'll have to imagine the creek. And the dirt too, I suppose.
That's what I mean by helping me out. But first, you'll have
to imagine the Liquor Store.

Lights indicate a change of scene, into the world of the play, in front of the
Liquor Store.

Thunder rolls in the distance. A light rain begins to fall. McAllister stands
with his reporter's steno pad and a pen at the ready. He tries to stop Mike.

Hey there, hey there! I'm taking a poll for the local paper.

Mike: I'm sorry.

McAllister: Oh come on. Your bottle of rye will still be there when you're done talking.

Mike: Not much point. I don't really live around here anymore.

McAllister: Well, I'll be danged. Schmidt. Michael Schmidt, isn't it? You moved away back in the '90s.

Mike: Yeah. That's right. You're —

McAllister: McAllister.

Mike: You run the local paper, right? What's it called again?

McAllister: The Local Paper.

Mike: . . . Good name. I'm surprised you remember me.

McAllister: It's my business. First question —

Mike: I told you, I don't live —

McAllister: I need an outsider's opinion. First question: the new highway, good or bad?

Mike: That's easy. Good.

McAllister: Second question: what are you, an idiot? How can a four-lane highway that reroutes traffic from Main Street to the middle of nowhere possibly be good for the town?

Mike: All those construction workers have to —

McAllister: Sure, in the short term. But half the businesses in this town rely on providing service to traffic coming through.

Mike: The real estate prices will more than offset —

McAllister: A one-time bump in real estate prices is hardly compensation for driving customers away —

Mike, unwilling to listen to a lecture, shakes his head and enters the liquor store.

Where're you going? Mike? Mike?

Mike: Sounds like you don't need an opinion from an outsider after all.

McAllister (*to the audience*): I guess the thing about taking a poll is that people expect questions, not answers.

MUSIC: "WHITE TRASH"

Caroline exits the liquor store carrying a bottle of wine and a case of beer and crosses to the car where Johnny is waiting.

Ah. The heroes of our tale. Johnny Deere. And his wife Caroline.

McAllister (*singing*): When he met her she was a Beauty Queen
                        who wanted something more.
                        Now she's hanging out with him
                        in front of the liquor store.

Caroline puts the case of beer and bottle of wine in the back seat of the car, then sits down in the passenger seat.

Johnny (*singing*):   And it won't start when you shut it off,
                        so she has to get the beer.
                        She puts it in the backseat
                        and she quietly says to me:

Caroline (*singing*):   When exactly did we become white trash?
How come we got seven dogs living in the
    garage?
How come the only 8-track in our car is
    Johnny Cash?
When exactly did we become white trash?

Johnny (*singing*):   And she tells all our friends
that I've got my Ph.D.

Caroline (*spoken*):   But it stands for post-hole-digger.

McAllister (*singing*):   It ain't exactly a degree.

Johnny (*singing*):   But there's curtains on the windows
and we hardly watch TV.
And that double-wide is triple-wide
now that she's with me.

McAllister (*singing*):   And she says:

Caroline (*singing*):   When exactly did we become white trash?
How come we got seven dogs?
Who burned down the garage?
How come the only 8-track in our car is

Johnny (*singing*):   Johnny Cash?

Johnny & Caroline (*singing*): When exactly did we become white trash?

Johnny: One case?

Caroline: Maybe it'll help you cut down a bit.

Johnny: We're just gonna have to come back tomorrow.

Caroline: And then you can go in all by yourself.

Johnny: I got a bottle of rye at home.

Caroline: You're not that much fun to be around when you drink rye all weekend.

Johnny: Then how about another case of beer?

Caroline hesitates, then sighs and gets out, but Johnny remains inside the idling vehicle. McAllister intercepts Caroline before she enters the liquor store. Johnny peers impatiently.

McAllister: Caroline!

Caroline: Hello, Mac. Another survey?

McAllister: I'm tryin' to find out what people think about the new highway.

Caroline tosses off a comment as she enters the store.

Caroline: Why don't you just recycle what I said about those wind turbines?

McAllister: Wait. I actually want your opinion.

Caroline returns from the door slowly, suspiciously.

Caroline: My opinion?

McAllister: Yes.

Caroline: You've never asked my opinion before. About anything.

McAllister: What do you think?

Caroline: It'll cut down on speeding, I suppose.

McAllister: Speeding!? Are you seriously —

Caroline: I thought you wanted my opinion?

McAllister reluctantly holds his tongue.

> Remember when the Mulligan boy was killed? That guy was going, like, ninety, right down Main Street.

McAllister: Errr. I'll have to work that into my editorial.

Caroline: And it might provide some jobs for folk around here.

McAllister: What about the jobs it'll take away?

Caroline: I — what?

Johnny: Caroline!

McAllister: We're about halfway between the city and the lake, so by the time most people get here they need to stretch their legs, buy some gas, grab a coffee. Maybe stop in at Elinor's Antique Shop over there.

Caroline: Only if they're really bored.

McAllister: Sure —

Caroline: Have you seen the stuff in there? None of it's antique. It's junk that she rubbed with sandpaper so it looks "distressed."

McAllister: They put a highway out there, it'll suck the life right out of this town.

Johnny (*from the car*): Caroline!

Caroline (*to Johnny*): Hold your frickin' horses!

McAllister: You ever been to Duncaster down south?

Caroline: No.

McAllister: Of course not.

MUSIC: "WHITE ROSE"

McAllister (*singing*): Well the whole town came out to watch
                  the day they paved the parking lot.
                  Somebody hung a ribbon up
                  and then they cut it down.
                  And that big White Rose up on that sign
                  Was the innocence in all our lives.
                  You could see its neon lights
                  half a mile out.
                  Gas was fifty cents a gallon
                  and they'd put it in for you
                  and they'd pump your tires and check your oil
                  and wash your windows too.
                  And we'd shine those cars as bright as bright
                  and we'd go park underneath that light
                  and stare out at the prairie sky;
                  There was nothing else to do.
                  But now there's plywood for glass
                  where the windows all got smashed.
                  And there's just a chunk of concrete
                  where those old pumps used to stand.
                  There's a couple of cars half out of the ground
                  and that oil sign still spins 'round and 'round.
                  But I guess the White Rose filling station's
                       just a memory now. . .

McAllister, Mike & Caroline (*singing*): And that neon sign was the
heart and soul of that old one-horse town
and it's like it lost its will to live
the day they shut it down.

McAllister & Caroline (*singing*): And now there's plywood for glass
where the windows all got smashed.
And there's just a chunk of concrete
where those old pumps used to stand.
There's a couple of cars half out of the ground
and that oil sign still spins 'round and 'round.
But I guess the White Rose filling station's
just a memory now. . .
I guess the White Rose filling station's just a
memory now. . .

Caroline: That's so sad. You figure that could happen here?

McAllister: I *know* it will happen here.

Johnny (*from the car*): Caroline!

Caroline: Okay, okay, I'll get your beer.

McAllister: What's that all about?

Caroline: Ask him. Go ahead. Find out why he can't even shut Lucille
off.

Caroline goes inside the liquor store. McAllister approaches
Johnny's side of the car, protecting himself from the rain.

McAllister: Johnny.

Johnny: Mac.

McAllister: Everything all right?

Johnny: Wish it would stop raining.

McAllister: First it doesn't rain for weeks, then it won't stop. Seedlings just barely get started, then they gotta learn how to swim.

Johnny: You worried about that creek at all?

McAllister: That creek hasn't flooded since 1975. Mind you, it hasn't rained this much since 1975.

Johnny: If it floods that lower field, that's most of my harvest.

McAllister: Relax. It won't flood unless they open the spillway up on Miller's Ridge. And they aren't going to do that without warning everyone downstream. At the very least they'll call me and have me put a notice in The Local Paper.

Johnny: Huh.

Pause.

You seen a coyote running about?

McAllister: Out at our place, you mean?

Johnny: I lost a few chickens.

McAllister: You figure a coyote got them?

Johnny: Chickens don't just wander away, Mac. Not if you feed 'em right. Can I borrow your rifle?

McAllister: Mine? What did you do with your Dad's rifle?

Johnny: I got rid of it when the government said I had to pay $50 a year for something I wasn't usin'. Is it still in your shed?

McAllister: Maybe. I don't really recall. Old Lucille here running all right?

Johnny: Caroline just can't leave it alone for one second.

McAllister: What's Caroline got to do with it?

Johnny: She told you to ask me about Lucille, didn't she?

McAllister: What's up with the car?

Johnny: It won't start if I shut it off. I gotta get under the hood. Caroline hates it because she's gotta work the starter. And all she does is flood it. And of course it's too much trouble for her to get the beer for a change.

McAllister: So. . . everything's all right then?

Johnny (*sighing*): Same as ever.

Caroline comes out of the liquor store with a second case of beer at the same time as Mike. He holds the door for her.

Mike: Let me get that for you. Caroline? Caroline Gamble? It's Mike Schmidt. You probably don't remember but we went to high school together.

Caroline: Oh, hi! Of course I remember you.

Mike: Gosh, I haven't seen you since prom.

Caroline: Before that really. I never made it to prom.

Mike: Oh, right. Because of the... er... trouble. What have you been up to?

Caroline: I'm married.

Mike: Of course you are. Anybody I know?

Caroline: Johnny Deere.

Mike: Really?

Caroline: Yeah.

Mike: Johnny D. That's — Well, I wouldn't have thought it, is all.

Caroline: Me neither.

Mike: So you're both living out on his place? Maybe I'll drop by sometime.

Caroline: Sure.

Caroline starts towards the car. She turns back.

Or maybe see you in town. I'm seeing a movie tonight. I'll be at the Legion after.

Mike: Right. See you there. Maybe.

Caroline: Maybe.

Caroline crosses to the car where Johnny is waiting and puts the second case of beer in the back seat.

Johnny: Was that Mike Schmidt you were talkin' to?

Caroline: What about it?

Johnny: Did he say what he's in town for?

Caroline: No. Let's go before this piece of crap stalls again.

Johnny puts the car into gear and it reverses away.

MUSIC: "WHITE TRASH" (REPRISE)

Johnny (*singing*):   And she tells all our friends
that I've got my Ph.D.

Caroline (*spoken*):   But it stands for post-hole-digger
it ain't exactly a degree.

Johnny (*singing*):   But there's curtains on the windows
and we hardly watch TV.
And that double-wide is triple-wide
now that she's with me.
And she says:

Caroline (*singing*):   When exactly did we become white trash?
How come we got seven dogs,
Who burned down the garage?
How come the only 8-track in our car is

Johnny (*singing*):   Johnny Cash?

Caroline (*singing*):   When exactly did we become white trash?

Johnny & Caroline (*singing*): When exactly did we become white trash?

MUSIC: "MCALLISTER'S THEME"

McAllister is back to his Narrator role, with appropriate lighting.
In the background Johnny and Caroline arrive at their farm and
unload the car, not speaking to each other.

McAllister: They say: "In the country everyone knows everyone else's business." But that's bull-roar. When your nearest neighbour is a mile or two up the road, you can pretty much chop a cord of wood in the buff.

Johnny and Caroline, they don't get to pick and choose what they share with their neighbour. This is their house, and this here, not near twenty feet away, is mine. Peculiar thing, a pair of houses so close together in the middle of the country. I won't go into the story of the old man who built them, of the two loving brothers who lived there and the wedge that came between them. That's a story for another time. And frankly, it still gets me riled up.

Just trust me when I tell ya that it's pretty near impossible to hide what goes on behind closed doors from a neighbour that practically lives in your front frickin' yard.

MUSIC: "YELLOW BARLEY STRAW"

All (*singing*):   He's got a heart made of Yellow Barley Straw

The garage. Rain drums on the corrugated metal roof. Johnny is
repairing a lawnmower engine. Caroline enters the garage holding
a few sheets of paper in her hands. She is wearing a slinky dress
and bright-coloured makeup.

Caroline: I just got off the phone with Johnstone's.

Johnny: What'd they want?

Caroline: Their money, apparently. Mavis says we haven't made a
    payment since February.

Johnny: They give you a month's grace.

Caroline: It's June now.

Johnny: I know what month it is, Caroline.

Caroline: Says she wouldn't mind if it wasn't for the fact we still owe
    for that diesel from March.

Johnny: Huh.

Caroline: "Huh"? That's all you have to say? "Huh"?

Johnny: I have to get this mower fixed for Jim.

Pause.

Caroline: I told her I was sure there was some mistake. So I went
    downstairs to that rat's nest you call an office —

Johnny: Just leave that stuff alone —

Caroline: — and here it is, right on the bottom of the pile. Third notice,
    overdue.

Johnny: It was January, Caroline. We had to have heat.

Caroline (*sarcastically*): You'll never guess what was right on top.
    Phone bill. Two months due. And what's this? Visa. That's
    over a thousand dollars, Johnny.

Johnny: I got a system down there in that office and —

Caroline: What kind of system is that, Johnny? Putting overdue bills on the bottom of the pile until they feel sorry for themselves and just slink away all on their own?

Johnny: You can't get blood out of a stone, Caroline. I can't pay them with money we don't have.

Caroline flips through the pages and holds one up. She marches down the steps and waves it under his nose.

Caroline: This one's been paid.

Johnny: That's seed, Caroline. God willing, it stops raining someday and it gets a chance to grow.

Caroline: You can pay this, but not these?

Johnny: Nothin' goes into the ground, nothin' goes into the bank.

Caroline: The Seed Mill will wait. Bell won't wait.

Johnny: I see Doug MacIntosh every week.

Caroline: Is that what it takes, Johnny? You just deal with whatever's right in your face? There's over three hundred dollars of interest here alone.

Johnny: What're you wearin'?

Caroline: I'm going out with Janet. I told you that weeks ago.

Johnny: Is that. . . blush?

Caroline: It's called makeup, Johnny. Women wear it when they want to look "made up."

Johnny: You're going to the movies.

Caroline: We might go out for a drink. We haven't decided.

Johnny: Janet Manning hasn't decided if she's having a drink or going to a movie?

Caroline: No.

Johnny: I got a hundred dollars right here that says Janet Manning has every night scheduled between now and Labour Day.

Caroline: Don't change the subject, Johnny.

Johnny: If I call right now, she's going to tell me she's getting ready to go out to a movie tonight?

Caroline: She better be. I don't want to be late.

Johnny: Yeah. She better be.

Pause.

Caroline: Do you want to talk about something?

Johnny: No.

Caroline: No. You never want to talk about anything, do you? We're in deep trouble here, Johnny.

Johnny: We'll get the bills —

Caroline: I'm not talkin' about the bills, you jackass.

Caroline starts to exit. She comes back.

You made me a promise. And you're not living up to it.

Caroline stalks off.

Johnny: Don't take my car.

Caroline (*going*): Wouldn't dream of it. I want something that'll start.

MUSIC: "SPOOKIN' THE HORSES"

Johnny grabs his bottle of rye from its hiding place in his workbench and pours himself a glass. Both the bottle and the glass are familiar friends. Johnny doesn't like to drink from the bottle, but he doesn't want to wipe the glass out with his dirty cloth either. He settles on blowing the fuzz that has collected on the bottom of the glass and wiping it out with his cleanest finger. He's left his mix inside the house, but he doesn't really care.

Johnny (*singing*): You're spookin' the horses
They're wild and they're scared
Well, that bright-coloured makeup
and those clothes that you wear
And I seen you dancin'
Last night 'neath the tree
You're spookin' the horses
And you're scaring me.

Caroline is dancing beneath the tree in the moonlight. It's a slow dance, with her back to the audience. Desire runs through the muscles of her shoulders as she hugs herself for comfort. She also has a glass, filled with white wine, that she manages to make seem like it's balanced on her hip while she sways to the music.

Caroline (*singing*): Where the road meets the highway
those bright city lights
must have shone through my windshield
and got into my eyes
And I guess I thought
that they'd set me free

Johnny (*singing*):   You're spookin' the horses
and you're scarin' me.

Caroline is alone, but she knows there's a man somewhere watching her.
It isn't Johnny. And she doesn't mind.

Caroline (*singing*):   I'm not tying my hair back anymore
And I'm wearing dresses like I never before
And I'm driving faster than you've ever seen

Johnny (*singing*):   You're spookin' the horses
and you're scarin' me.

Mike hands her another glass of wine. Is this just an actor handing a fellow
performer a prop? Or is he part of the scene? And is that a little bit of
flirtation that passed between them? Or just a friendly smile?

I can hear the gears grinding
Where you make the turn
And up on the skyline
Those headlights just burn
And the horses go runnin'
And my heart just screams.

You're spookin' the horses
and you're scarin' me.
You're spookin' the horses
and you're scarin' me.

Lights fade on Caroline and Mike. . . and on Johnny and his bottle of rye.

McAllister: I've seen that boy out of a lot of jams in my time. I've done
my share for him. And his father. . .

MUSIC: UNDERSCORING BEGINS.

At the risk of steering us all into the ditch, I'm gonna take a wide cut across the headland and turn about fifteen years in the other direction. Try to keep up. This is where you need to use that imagination I was talking about earlier. The houses are the same, but my brother who was living here had passed on. And in his place, a single father off the boat from Holland. He set up a small motors repair shop right next door.

Lights on Hendrik, Johnny's father.

MUSIC: "SMALL MOTORS"

McAllister (*speaking*): He wore railroad coveralls
with his name written on his chest.
We talked Model A's and T's
While he rolled cigarettes.
And we'd get lost inside our thoughts,
And we'd let those tanks run dry.
And one by one those little engines'd
Sputter and they'd die.

McAllister (*speaking*) & **All** (*underscoring*): And he liked small motors,
flywheels on the side,
single piston engines made out of cast iron.
He liked small motors.
He'd start 'em one by one.
We'd stand around and we'd listen
to them little engines run.

A young Johnny (maybe fifteen) emerges in a rage, slamming the screen door behind him. Hendrik is close behind him.

Johnny: I can so!

Hendrik: Such en mighty big car. Never run.

Johnny: I'll make it run. You'll see.

Hendrik: Much water flow through de Rhine before dat hapen. En big car is not en small motor.

Johnny: Just watch me.

Hendrik: Small motor first. Den maybe en tractor. Only after — maybe — en mighty big car.

Johnny: Other kids my age have cars.

Hendrik: You have not even en license.

Johnny: I will in a year. I can drive it then.

Hendrik: Study at de school. Dat's what your mother wants you to do.

Johnny: How do you know what my mother wants? She's dead.

Hendrik slaps Johnny. Johnny is about to hit back with the wrench in his hand. They stare each other down. Johnny throws his wrench on the ground and exits. Hendrik picks up the wrench and stares at it.

McAllister: Teenagers. They know it all at that age.

Hendrik: Never speaked to my Vader like dat. Never. Hard just me since his Moeder, she passed.

McAllister: Teenagers are like horses. You give them a little lead and they tend not to pull as hard. You might try cutting Johnny a little slack.

Hendrik (*turning on him*): Enough from you. You have not even en wife. Not even en children. Can't even fix own fence.

McAllister (*to audience*): Yep. Hendrik was a real Canadian immigrant success story. If only he hadn't been such a grumpy bastard.

Hendrik: Dis fixed? All my cow will get out and you fault. You fix.

McAllister: Later. I need to cover the auction for the paper.

Hendrik: Auction?

McAllister: Lindstrom over on the fifth concession died last month. He was an old-timer, so it'll be a lot of antiques. There's bound to be a bargain.

Hendrik: Bargain?! Johannes. Come.

Hendrik looks at McAllister expectantly. He rubs his hands together.

Murky water make good fishing.

McAllister hadn't intended to invite Hendrik, but now that he has invited himself along, McAllister doesn't quite know how to extricate himself from the situation.

McAllister: My brother used to say nothing brings a town together like a church picnic. But that was just another stupid thing he used to say. A church picnic is just a bunch of Anglicans drinking tea with other Anglicans and Presbyterians eating sandwiches with other Presbyterians, and Pentecostals doing... whatever it is Pentecostals do with other Pentecostals.

MUSIC: UNDERSCORING BEGINS.

Forget the churches. What binds a town together is faith. Faith that they can find a good deal.

Let's use that imagination again, if you got any left.

The furniture's over here, a big pile of it on the front lawn. Some of it's kinda cheap, plastic lawn chairs and the like. The kitchen stuff, silverware, pots and pans and appliances, are all over here.

And over here is the farm equipment. This is where all the farmers are gathered. And most of them are gathered around one old tractor. Hendrik saw that tractor as soon as he and Johnny pulled up.

MUSIC: UNDERSCORING TRANSFORMS INTO "JOHN DEERE B."

McAllister (*singing*): Well I watched him from the window
as he parked across the lane.
His face was red and sunburned,
his clothes were torn and stained.
He wasn't a collector,
he hadn't come here for a bargain.
He needed that old tractor
to farm his old farm.
It was a John Deere B:
with a row crop front end;
hand crank and a flywheel;
the original paint.
But it won't work another field,
farm another farm.
Some restaurant down in Oshawa should
park it on its lawn.

Johnny: I don't want a stupid tractor.

Hendrik: First — tractor you will learn fix. Same as mighty big car.

Johnny: Oh yeah? If I get it started, will you buy that car for me?

Hendrik: Why car? When tractor you even cannot fix?

Johnny fiddles with the tractor until it roars to life.

McAllister (*singing*): I watched him check the oil,
      I watched him set the spark.
      He pulled on that old pump,
      until he finally got it started.
      He listened to the motor,
      then he set the touch.
      When he got it goin'
      I watched him slowly smile.
      It was a

All (*singing*):   John Deere B:
      with a row crop front end;
      hand crank and a flywheel
      the original paint.
      But it won't work another field,
        farm another farm.
      Some museum up in Ottawa should
        park it on its lawn.

Hendrik: Ha! Good, Johannes! Good!

Johnny: So. You're going to buy me this tractor?

Hendrik: I thought car you want?

Johnny: You said, "First tractor. Then car."

Hendrik: "Maybe car," I say. But for you tractor I buy. I promise.

MUSIC: UNDERSCORING CONTINUES.

Caroline provides the voice of the Auctioneer while McAllister and Johnny look idly on. Hendrik gets increasingly nervous as the bidding goes higher.

Auctioneer: Yew K! Here we go. They don't make 'em like this anymore. A John Deere B! I want a bid, I want a bid, what're you gonna bid, what're you gonna bid? Who'll give me ten thousand — ten thousand dollars? I want a bid, I want a bid, Nine! Nine. Who's gonna start at nine? Come on, folks. Built in the Heartland of America.

MUSIC: "THE TRACTOR AUCTION" *

Johnny (*singing*):   Don't let 'er go.
It's almost yer duty.
The oil pressure's fine,
she's a hard-workin' cutie.
In the blink of an eye,
I'll be riding that beauty
up and down the lane

Auctioneer: I want a bid, I want a bid, What're you gonna bid, what're you gonna bid? Six. Who'll start us a six. Six? Six? Six? Four thousand. It's a steal at four.

Hendrik: One thousand.

---

* *This portion of the musical number, entitled "The Tractor Auction," has been composed by David Archibald. It is embedded within the Fred Eaglesmith song "John Deere B."*

Auctioneer: One thousand from the back. Gotta start somewhere. I got a bid, I got a bid What're you gonna bid, what're you gonna bid I got one thousand dollars. Looking for one and a half — one and a half — one and a half. ONE AND A HALF! Lookin' for two — two — two thousand.

Hendrik: Two thousand.

Auctioneer: TWO! Thank you, sir. I want two and a half — two and a half — two and a half.

Johnny (*singing*):   Yeah, look at her there.
She's one of a kind.
We gotta take 'er home.
Don't change your mind.

Hendrik: You might even take a little time to thank me one day.

Auctioneer: TWO AND A HALF! Give me three, three, three thousand. Look at this machine! Got two and a half, got two and a half. Gimme three, three, three.

Johnny (*singing*):   She's a tiny bit worn,
from the dirt and the dust,
she's got a lot of class,
and a touch of rust,

Hendrik & Johnny (*singing*): but that logo on her side
Is the one to trust.
She's a CLASSIC!

Auctioneer: Got three. Got three. Gimme three and a half, three and a half, three and a half. I got a bid, I got a bid, What're you gonna bid, what're you gonna bid? THREE AND A HALF!

The bidding continues underneath.

MUSIC: UNDERSCORING TRANSFORMS INTO "JOHN DEERE B."

McAllister (*singing*): When the bidding started
I saw him twitch his eye
Then I saw them narrow
When the price went too high.

*Hendrik looks at Johnny. He doesn't say a word. They both return to
Hendrik's car and depart.*

He turned and looked a couple times
before he got into his car.
Quietly he turned around
and drove out of the yard.

Underscoring continues.

Auctioneer: I got a bid, I got a bid, what're you gonna bid, what're
you gonna bid?

Bidder: Four.

Auctioneer: I got four. Gimme four and a half — four and a half —
four and a half. Four and a quarter, four and a quarter. John
Deere B. Four and a quarter. Got four thousand. Going once,
twice...

McAllister: Five thousand!

Auctioneer: Sold! Congratulations, Mr. McAllister.

McAllister: You see, the thing about an auction is that one does tend
to get carried away by the excitement of it all. I knew how
much Johnny wanted that tractor.

*The sound of an old tractor sputtering to life and driving down the road.
Johnny and Hendrik come out of the house and stare at the tractor.*

MUSIC: UNDERSCORING TRANSFORMS INTO "JOHN DEERE B."

Hendrik is so pleased he wants to give McAllister a hug, but he's just not that kind of man. McAllister knows this and doesn't expect any thanks. He just hands Hendrik the keys. Hendrik nods.

McAllister (*singing*): Well, he watched me from the window
as I parked across the lane.
His face was red and sunburned,
his clothes were old and stained.
He wasn't a collector,
he wouldn't put it on display.
You'd see him on that tractor
Each and every day.
It was a

All (*singing*): John Deere B:
with a row crop front end;
hand crank and a flywheel;
the original paint.
And it will work another field,
farm another farm.
No museum up in Ottawa's gonna park it
on its lawn.

McAllister (*singing*): No museum up in Ottawa is gonna park it
on its lawn!

Hendrik smiles at Johnny for the only time in the play.

About the only thing Johnny and his Dad could agree on in all the time I knew them was that tractor.

Flashback ends.

MUSIC: "MCALLISTER'S THEME"

McAllister: I helped one relationship in that boy's life.

Lights on Caroline sitting at a stool by the bar.

> But I didn't figure there was much chance I'd be able to help this time. It was just coincidence that I had to go into town that night.

The twangy strains of a country band in a bar begin and transport us into the local watering hole. Mike comes over and starts talking with Caroline, in dumb show. Caroline invites him to sit down.

> Every good Canadian town has a Royal Canadian Legion: the kind of place where beer is served in mason jars, there's a vat of pickled eggs on the bar, and there's two kinds of music available on the jukebox: country *and* western.

McAllister sees Caroline and Mike. He sneaks close enough to eavesdrop without being noticed.

Mike: I have seen the future, etched in blue lines.

Caroline: You're clairvoyant, are you?

Mike (*nodding*): Highways department. Blue lines on a topographical map of this township that show where this highway everyone's talking about is going to be built. I saw it when I worked for the province.

Caroline: No one knows where it's going to be built.

Mike: I do. I worked for the land acquisitions department.

McAllister leans in and interrupts. Caroline and Mike immediately put more space between them.

McAllister: If the government is going to go around expropriating farms, it seems to me that there'd likely be a little more formal process involved than just sending out some guy in a nice truck.

Mike: I *used* to work for the government. And I'm not expropriating anything. I'm offering a fair price.

McAllister: And is that legal? You using what you know from working for the government to make a quick buck?

Mike: There's lots of different definitions of what's legal.

McAllister: No there's not. But there *are* a lot of different definitions of who's a criminal... and who actually ends up in jail.

McAllister stands up and leaves, rudely. Caroline shouts after him.

Caroline: Mac! Mac!

Mike: Do I look like a criminal to you, Caroline?

Caroline: A little better dressed, maybe.

Mike: Why thank you. How about that dance you promised me?

Caroline: I never promised you any dance.

Mike: Yes you did. Back in high school, you promised me one dance at the prom. And you never showed.

Caroline: I'm a married woman, Michael Schmidt.

Mike (*holding out his hand*): Then there's no harm in one dance.

Caroline: How about you give me a smoke instead?

Mike: We can't smoke inside anymore. Even at the Legion.

Caroline: It's a nice night.

Caroline leads the way outside. Mike follows.

Mike: I think I have a light in my truck.

Caroline: Whoa. Nice truck there, Mike. How's it drive?

Mike: Like a dream. Four-wheel drive, ABS brakes. Great in winter driving conditions. Not great on gas, though.

Caroline: What's it haul? Maybe a ton? Two?

Mike: You know, I'm not sure.

Caroline: Is that the one with the anti-sway thingamadoodle? So your load don't get out of control on you when a gust of wind comes up?

Mike: I think they mentioned that at the dealership. Yeah.

Caroline: You do a lot of hauling up there in Toronto, then?

Mike: Not really.

Caroline: Must have some occasion. Basement renos. Rebuilding the back deck. Treehouse for the kids.

Mike: That's not really my thing.

Caroline: Take stuff to the dump at least?

Mike: The city picks it all up. Curbside. You know.

Caroline: So it's just a tall car as far as your concerned, then?

Mike: An *expensive* tall car.

MUSIC: "I WANNA BUY YOUR TRUCK"

Caroline starts to seduce Mike with the lyrics of the song

Caroline (*singing*):   So many mornings, so many days. . .
I just dream out my window, about going away.
I dream of white lines, cigarette stops,
broken-down shoulders, rusty old trucks.

Caroline & Mike (*singing*): I wanna buy your truck:
I don't like what I'm doing,
I wanna give it up.
I wanna try something else.
I like the way that it shines. . .
Hey, I'm really stuck
in this life of mine.
I wanna buy your truck.

Caroline (*singing*):   And the dust devil drive shafts,
the mirrored mirages,
the oil-can silhouettes, falling-down garages,
Chrome-grille reflections, just out of the lights,
onto the pavement, into the night. . .

Caroline & Mike (*singing*): I wanna buy your truck:
I don't like what I'm doing,
I wanna give it up.
I wanna try something else.
I like the way that it shines. . .
Hey, I'm really stuck
in this life of mine.
I wanna buy your truck.

Caroline (*singing*):   When I get to the ocean, I'm gonna drive right in.
And when it stalls, I'm gonna get out and swim.

Caroline & Mike (*singing*): I wanna buy your truck:
        I don't like what I'm doing,
        I wanna give it up.
        I wanna try something else.
        I like the way that it shines...
        Hey, I'm really stuck
        in this life of mine.

Caroline (*singing*): I wanna buy your truck
        I like the way that it shines ...
        Hey, I'm really stuck
        in this life of mine.
        I wanna buy your truck.
        I'm stuck in this life of mine
        I wanna...

Pause. Caroline kisses Mike.

MUSIC: DISSONANT UNDERSCORING.

Elsewhere, that same night. The rain has stopped, but the air still feels wet. Crickets fill the summer air with the incessant sound of their chirruping. Nocturnal tree frogs bleat a call to their wayward mates. Johnny is now asleep at the table, his bottle of rye whiskey in front of him. There is a noise outside. The barking of the dogs wakes Johnny up with a start.

Johnny: Wa' that? Caroline? Tha' you?

Johnny rubs the sleep from his eyes and moves to the window. He doesn't see anything but he's sure he heard something. He steps outside into the night. Silence.

Something is different now. Even the crickets and tree frogs are mysteriously still. Johnny shakes his head and focuses on the strangeness of it all.

Something moves over by the old John Deere and he jumps.

Who's that? Someone there? Caroline, is that you?

Mike emerges from behind the tractor. We're not sure if this is a dream or not, but we're pretty certain that Mike isn't real.

Mike: Have you had a chance to think about our conversation from last week, Johnny D?

Johnny: You again. What're you doin' here in the middle of the night?

Mike: Maybe I'm not here. Maybe this is just a dream. Maybe I'm out with your wife.

Johnny: Quit talkin' about my wife.

Mike: If you want. It's your dream. Did you tell Caroline about our conversation?

Johnny: No.

Mike: Why not?

Johnny: I guess I'm afraid she'd say yes.

Mike: If you won't sell, I'm sure it's only a matter of time before those bills catch up to you.

Johnny: You know what I been thinkin'?

Mike: No. What've you been thinking?

THE UNDERSCORING TURNS INTO MUSIC: A DISSONANT VERSION OF "TIME TO GET A GUN."

Johnny (*speak-singing*): My neighbour's car got stole last week
right outta his driveway.

Mike: Is that so?

Johnny (*speak-singing*): We heard the dogs a-barkin';
we never paid them any mind.
Caroline says she's gonna lock the door
from now on when we go away.
And I been walking around this farm
a-wondering if it's time. . .
Time to get a gun.

MUSIC: DISSONANT UNDERSCORING ENDS.

McAllister: Johnny was twenty-seven when he met Caroline. She
was seventeen. She was set to graduate high school. He did
better with his hands than his brains. He showed us all just
how much better when he took the rusted-out shell of a 1952
Cadillac convertible and not only made it run again, he made
it the envy of the whole town.

*Flashback: Johnny and Caroline are fifteen years younger. And so is
Lucille, the mighty big car that threatened to stall in front of the liquor
store earlier in Act One.*

Johnny: Twenty-eight feet from bumper to bumper. The last of the
sweet old-time gas-guzzlers. Hard to drive, harder to park.
Elvis had one and so did Hank. It doesn't look like money,
it looks like the bank.

Caroline: They say that when a guy has to have a mighty big car, it's because he's got a mighty small something in another department.

Johnny looks at Caroline, in shock. No one — especially a girl — has ever spoken to him this way. Far from reacting badly, he is amused at her audacity. It's nighttime, and there is a party going on offstage, out by the gravel pit. The rest of the high school gang is hanging out down there. Caroline has come up the hill to meet the older guys.

Johnny: That so? And what're you drivin'?

Caroline: I'm not driving anything. I get boys like you to drive me wherever I want.

Johnny: Not talkin' like that you don't.

Caroline: I'm Caroline.

Johnny: Johnny D.

Caroline: You gonna offer a girl one of those Molsons, Johnny D?

Johnny: I don't give beer to underage girls. But I'm sure someone down by the fire will.

Caroline doesn't go anywhere. She's intrigued, and not about to be intimidated.

Caroline: Come on, I graduate high school next week.

Johnny: Well, excuuuuuse me. So, what're you doing up here with the grown-ups?

Caroline: Maybe I like it here.

Johnny: Wearing city jeans like those? You gotta be pretty sick of this small town already.

Caroline: Wherever you go, there you are.

Johnny: Huh?

Caroline: It means you can't run away from who you are. It's Buddhist. We learned it in Social Studies.

Johnny: I think I remember that class.

Caroline (*sizing him up*): You work real hard at your image, don't you?

Johnny: So?

Caroline: Wherever you go, there you are.

Pause while Johnny considers just how he's going to use his carefully chosen words to take her down a peg or two.

Johnny: Lemme see if I can figure out *your* image. Good girl in junior high. But then came high school. Smoking behind the bleachers. Getting kissed by the senior boys. Breaking Single Mom's heart. She sent you to Daddy, straighten you out. Except Daddy's Little Girl has him wrapped around her little finger.

Caroline: Who told you that?

Johnny: It's in your eyes. The way you walk.

Caroline: That's a nice way to talk to a girl you just met.

Johnny takes a swig of his beer and doesn't see Caroline wipe away a tear. Or at least he pretends he doesn't.

Johnny: Wherever you go, there you are.

Caroline: I guess I deserved that.

Johnny holds out his bottle for a toast.

Johnny: Truce?

Caroline: Mine's empty. I'm going to need another from your back
seat if I'm going to cheers you.

Pause, while Johnny absorbs the hint buried within this statement.

Johnny: Lucille's not meant for sitting. She's meant for riding.

Caroline (*leaning in suggestively*): Then maybe you should take me
for a ride.

Johnny opens the car door for her, and tumbles in after her.

MUSIC: "BENCH SEAT BABY"

Johnny (*singing*):   Well I know you're used to those little sport jobs
with the console in between;
bold-faced leather, fancy headrest,
a pocket for your cold cream.
I know you're used to staring out the window
watching the world go by.
Well, it's a different kind of automobile,
It's a different kind of ride.

It's got a bench seat baby
It's got a bench seat baby
It's got a bench seat baby
You don't have to sit over there.

I know you're used to them little dance tunes
cranking out of the player.
Here's a lesson in country and western
It's gonna drive you crazy.
So undo your jacket, lay back your head,
won't you relax just a little?
And unless you got somebody else coming,
slide over into the middle.

*Caroline laughs and shakes her head at him. But she snuggles up next to
Johnny anyway. She joins in the chorus.*

Johnny & Caroline (*singing*): It's got a bench seat baby
It's got a bench seat baby
It's got a bench seat baby
You don't have to sit over there.

Johnny (*singing*):   Well, it's five feet from inseam to inseam.
I had it custom corduroyed.
And there's no reason why it needs to recline,
it was made for a girl and a boy.

Johnny & Caroline (*singing*): It's got a bench seat baby
It's got a bench seat baby
It's got a bench seat baby
You don't have to sit over there.

Johnny (*singing*):	**Caroline** (*singing*):
It's got a bench seat baby	It's a mighty big car
It's got a bench seat baby	It's a mighty big car

Johnny (*singing*):   It's got a bench seat baby
You don't have to sit over there

Johnny & Caroline (*singing*):   It's got a bench seat baby
You don't have to sit over there.

Caroline and Johnny kiss. Car headlights illuminate the cab.
The sound of a car horn causes Johnny to straighten the wheel
without breaking the kiss. Lights fade.

MUSIC: UNDERSCORING BEGINS.

McAllister: There's a place out in the country where couples go to be alone called "Kissing Cliff." Johnny and Caroline didn't bother to go there. They parked their car out near Johnny's house, overlooking the creek and the lower field.

Caroline: . . .There's an entire religion based on sitting quietly and not thinking so much. Isn't that cool?

McAllister: The headlights illuminated those tender shoots, struggling to make their way in the world, marching in endless rows into the future.

Caroline: . . . And those temples — they're cute! Like tiny little houses for tiny little monks. . .

McAllister: Johnny and Caroline strode like giants amongst that field of potential. I saw it all from my kitchen window.

Johnny and Caroline walk through a cornfield, where the seedlings are no higher than their ankles, hand in hand.

Caroline: I think they have a kind of temple in the city. I'm going to check it out when I get back.

Johnny: You're going back to the city?

Pause.

Caroline: I was supposed to be the Prom Princess.

Johnny (*mocking*): Oh my God! I'm holding hands with the *Prom* Queen!

Caroline: Not the Prom Queen but, you know, the Princess.

Johnny: Oh my God! I'm holding hands with the second-in-command to the Prom Queen!

Caroline: Stop it. Not even a Princess anymore. I had to forfeit my tiara or whatever.

Johnny (*still mocking*): What'd ya do?

Pause. Caroline is trying to stop the tears. Johnny drops all of his mocking and turns serious.

What'd you do?

Caroline: They caught me drinking at the school dance. It was nothing worse than what the other girls were doing.

Johnny: How'd they catch you?

Caroline: I was passed out on the lawn. They had to make an example out of someone. So I got suspended.

Johnny: Oh. That sucks.

Caroline: It really sucks. I was on the decorating committee.

Caroline is crying.

I organized this whole Asian theme. Like in that Social Studies class. I got everybody to make these Buddhist temples out of papier-mâché. I was gonna hang them from the ceiling on little strings. It's stupid. But I really liked them.

Johnny: That's not stupid. It sounds nice. Really nice.

Johnny lets her put her head on his shoulder.

Passing out drunk on the lawn at a school dance. . . that's stupid.

Caroline laughs. She looks up at Johnny and smiles. His sense of humour is just what she needs right now. They keep walking down the row of corn into the darkness, like ghosts. McAllister looks down the rows after them.

McAllister: The next weekend was prom.

Hendrik is working on a motor in the shop. Johnny approaches sheepishly.

Johnny: Vader.

Hendrik: Finally, returns the Son Prodigal. Maybe now that generator he will fix?

Johnny: Vader. De wind wait uit een heel andere hoek.*

Hendrik looks up from his labour, concerned.

I need your help.

---

*   *Translation: "The wind blows from another corner." Meaning: "The situation has changed."*

McAllister: Come prom night, Johnny drove Caroline back to the field. The sun was just starting to set, so it was kind of hard to make out the table standing in the middle of the field.

Lights on a table and two chairs sitting in the middle of a vast cornfield, surrounded by tender corn shoots. McAllister shows us the place setting, like a maitre d'.

It was set with a white tablecloth, silverware and wine glasses. An appetizer in Tupperware. Soup in a thermos. And here — wrapped in tinfoil to keep it warm — "Macaroni Dorate."

Johnny (*to Caroline, sheepishly*): That's Italian for Kraft Dinner.

A dozen papier-mâché Buddhist temples descend from the ceiling. Each of them is lit from within by a tiny twinkling light.

McAllister: It was Hendrik that flipped the switch. Then we both made ourselves scarce.

MUSIC: "WILDER THAN HER" (REPRISE)

Johnny (*singing*):   Well I'm wilder than her.
What else can I say?
But I guess that's why she fell in love with me.
She's a house on fire,
she's got all those charms,
I'm a house on fire too,
but I got four alarms.

And I'm wilder than her.
Drives her out of her mind.
I guess she thought that she was just
    one of a kind.
But she's summer storm,
I'm a hurricane.

One just blows through town,
    one blows the town away.
And I'm wilder than her.

When we go driving in our cars,
racing through the night.

Caroline (*singing*):   I can drive as fast as him.

Johnny (*singing*):   But she stops at all the lights.
    She thinks it's cause I'm crazy.

Caroline (*singing*):   I'm probably right.

Johnny (*singing*):   But I think that the reason is that I'm twice
    as wild.
    And I'm wilder than her.

Johnny & Caroline (*singing*): Drives her/me out of her/my mind.

Johnny (*singing*):   I guess she thought that she was just
    one of a kind.
    She's a summer storm,

Caroline (*singing*):   He's a hurricane.

Johnny (*singing*):   One just blows through town,

Johnny & Caroline (*singing*): One blows the town away.
    And I'm wilder than her.

Caroline (*singing*):   When he takes my hand
    and he looks me in the eye,
    I see something that I've never seen in my life.

Johnny (*singing*):   She takes the fire, turns it down low,

Caroline (*singing*):   He takes the night, and makes it not so cold.

Johnny (*singing*):   She takes the distance,

Johnny & Caroline (*singing*): Breaks it into miles.

Johnny (*singing*):   She makes my life just

Johnny & Caroline (*singing*): A little less wild.

Johnny (*singing*):   Cause I'm

Johnny & Caroline (*singing*): Wilder than her.

Johnny (*singing*):   Drives her

Johnny & Caroline (*singing*): Out of his mind.

Johnny (*singing*):   I guess she thought that
she was just one of a kind.
Johnny & Caroline (*singing*): But she's summer storm,

Johnny (*singing*):   I'm a hurricane.

Johnny & Caroline (*singing*): One just blows through town,

Johnny (*singing*):   one blows the town away.
And I'm wilder than her...

Johnny & Caroline (*singing*): And I'm wilder than her...
And I'm wilder than her.

They continue to dance as the light fades.

McAllister: They danced the night away in that field, until the sun came up the next day. The music from the car stereo kept me up most of the night. In the morning Lucille wouldn't start. Guess that stereo has a mighty big draw on that little-bitty battery. Caroline had to ride to town on the back of that old John Deere B. They reached the town limits just as all the other kids were stumbling home in their tuxedos and gowns: and there's the ex-Prom Princess on the back of a tractor. There's still debate over who had the better prom. But not in my mind.

Johnny and Caroline slowly lose their energy and buoyancy. Age and the care of years wears away their youth until they have once again become as they were through the first part of Act One.

Flashback ends.

MUSIC: "MCALLISTER'S THEME," NOW TURNED DISSONANT.

McAllister: But I guess it doesn't matter how they *were*. We're talking about how they *are*.

Thunder rolls in the distance. Lights. It's now suddenly the next day, a bright morning. Johnny is fiddling with a rifle. He accidentally swings it in McAllister's direction.

Watch where you're pointing that thing.

Johnny: You know what they say, Mac. "Guns don't kill people."

McAllister: People kill people. With guns. That mine?

Johnny: Yep.

McAllister: I haven't seen that for thirty-odd years.

Johnny: I figured it's time to get some protection. Deal with that damned coyote.

McAllister: So you thought you'd help yourself to my gun?

Johnny (*changing the subject*): Glad to see the sun for a change. I was getting worried about that spillway.

McAllister: I told you they'll have to contact the press before they —

Johnny: Yeah. Yeah. What you got under your arm this time?

McAllister hands Johnny the sheaf of papers.

McAllister: Petition. I'm collecting signatures against the new highway. Trying to tell the province that a highway is going to kill this community.

Johnny hands the sheaf of papers back.

Johnny: That's not what he tells me.

McAllister: Who's that?

Silence. Johnny does not answer.

Has someone been nosing around here, Johnny?

Johnny: Some fella from Toronto.

McAllister: What fella?

Johnny: Mike Whatshisname. Says the overpass is gonna go right through here.

McAllister: Well, that's not news, everybody —

Johnny: Right through *here*.

McAllister: Oh.

Johnny: He's offering to buy the place. Cash.

McAllister: You're a farmer, Johnny. Your father bought this land with money he scraped together —

Johnny: Land that ain't even fit for growin' rocks. I'm tired of farming with a pick and shovel.

McAllister: You're a farmer.

Johnny: Last year it woulda cost me more to harvest that lower field than I'd have gotten to sell it. I plowed it under and took the crop insurance.

McAllister: What does Caroline think about all this?

Johnny (*almost laughing*): Caroline? She went out on the town last night. All done up in her tightest dress.

McAllister: Yeah, I saw that.

Pause.

Johnny: Ya did?

McAllister: Yeah.

Johnny: Where'd you see that, exactly? The Legion, maybe?

McAllister: So she went out for a drink.

Johnny: Was she with anybody?

Just then a car pulls up the driveway offstage. McAllister is relieved. Johnny is not.

McAllister: Here she is now. So it was just... y'know... a heat-of-the-moment kind of thing. Don't you think?

Johnny: Yeah, thanks, Mac. Run along now.

McAllister: It's good she's back. Right?

Johnny picks up the gun again.

Johnny: Excuse us for a while. I gotta have a chat with my wife.

Johnny heads off towards the sound of the car. He stops just out of the light, in front of Caroline. They remain frozen, suspended in McAllister's story. McAllister turns towards the audience.

McAllister: Are you as worried as I was? Because, in this context, you can kind of see why there might be something to worry about. "Husband Shoots Wife... With Newspaperman's Gun." So, what I did next was kind of justified. Don't you think?

McAllister bends down behind the workbench in the drive shed so he cannot be seen by them, but he is perfectly visible to the audience. Johnny and Caroline re-enter the playing space.

Johnny: It's nearly noon.

Caroline: What, you think I don't own a watch?

Silence.

I was out with Janet.

Silence.

We had a few too many. I didn't think it was safe to drive.

Silence. Caroline picks up the empty bottle of rye.

Looks like you had a little party of your own.

Johnny: It's not a party if you're drinkin' by yourself.

Caroline: No. Then you're just a drunk.

Johnny: I'm not the one who couldn't come home last night.

Caroline: We were having a good time.

Johnny: Not with Janet Manning you weren't. McAllister saw you.

Pause.

Caroline: That nosy, inquisitive little —

Johnny: Aw, don't be too hard on him. He wouldn't tell me anything. I just wanted to see how worried you'd be if he had.

Pause.

So. Who *were* you with?

Caroline: I don't need to talk about it.

Johnny: Yes you do. I may be a lot of things. But I am still your husband. So you do need to talk about this.

Pause.

Caroline: We didn't go to a movie. We went to the bar.

Johnny: To hook up with Mike? Your old boyfriend?

Caroline: It was a coincidence. He bought me a drink.

Johnny: So you slept with him.

Caroline: I didn't.

Johnny: Don't lie to me, Caroline.

Pause.

Caroline: I slept with him.

Johnny: Jesus.

Caroline: Don't you swear at me.

Johnny: Well, who the hell else do you want me to swear at?

Caroline: I've been running a home, helping out on the farm, holding down a part-time job, and to top it all off, I'm responsible for the emotional health of this relationship too.

Johnny: Not this again.

Caroline: Yes, this again. I'm the one doing the heavy lifting, John.

Johnny: Is *that* what it's called these days.

Caroline: This is a great excuse for you to put up that brick wall you're so good at, isn't it?

Johnny thinks about striking out at something: maybe her.
He chooses to leave the garage instead. Caroline tries to stop him.

Where are you —?

Johnny: Don't. Just don't.

Johnny leaves the shed in a fit of fury and bumps into McAllister, who has been eavesdropping behind the workbench. MacAllister stands sheepishly.

Caroline: Why don't you just move in? It's a better view.

Johnny stalks off. McAllister begins to plead with Caroline, but in the end he hasn't the heart.

McAllister: Boy, do I feel like the world's worst neighbour. I, uh. . .
I. . .. I'll be going.

Caroline: I think you'd better.

McAllister starts to walk away. Johnny comes running back onstage and runs into the house.

We're either going to face what's going on —

Johnny: Not now.

Caroline: Well, then when?

MUSIC: UNDERSCORING BEGINS.

Johnny exits the house with his rubber boots and the portable telephone. Caroline follows him out. Johnny dials a number with one hand and tries to remove his shoes and put on his rubber boots as quickly as he can manage with the other.

Caroline: What's the matter now?

Johnny: The creek is flooded. The south field is under three feet of water.

McAllister: Three feet? Overnight? It's not even raining. How —?

Johnny waves to them to be quiet, so he can listen to the phone better. It's clearly some sort of recorded message. After a moment he slowly lowers the phone and turns to face McAllister.

Johnny: How do you think? They opened the spillway on Miller's Ridge.

No one speaks.

McAllister: That's. . . not possible. They would have called the paper.

Caroline turns and glares at him.

Caroline: Who reads your paper anymore, Mac? Honestly, how many readers do you have left? Is it any wonder they didn't bother to call the local rag?

McAllister is stunned. The truth in what Caroline has said has caused his world to come crumbling down. He hardly knows what to say.

McAllister (*whispering*): Paper.

Caroline: What?

McAllister: It's called The Local Paper. Not The Local Rag.

Caroline (*to Johnny*): How bad?

Johnny: The whole thing.

Caroline: All of it?

Johnny nods.

Think anything's gonna grow when it dries up?

Johnny shakes his head. Silence.

There is a ruckus offstage, in the henhouse. Johnny grabs the gun, thinking it could be the coyote. He sees it running off in the distance, and shoots at it. Many times, over and over again, grunting in fury each time. Pause.

McAllister gingerly takes the gun from Johnny. He offers him a guitar instead.

MUSIC: "TIME TO GET A GUN"

Johnny (*singing*):   I saw my wife get stole last night
right outta my driveway.
I heard the dogs a-barkin'
I never paid them any mind.
And maybe I am gonna lock the door
   from now on when I go away.
And I been walking around this farm
   a-wondering if it's time...

All (*singing*):   Time to get a gun.
That's what I been thinkin'.
I could afford one
if I did just a little less drinkin'.
Time to put somethin'
between me and the sun.
When the talkin' is over
it's time to get a gun.

Johnny (*singing*):   Last week a government man was there
when I walked outta my back door.
He said I'm sorry to bother you son,
but it don't matter anymore.
'Cause even while we're talkin'
right here where we stand,
they're makin' plans for a four-lane highway
and a big old overpass.

All (*singing*):   Time to get a gun.
That's what I been thinkin'.
I could afford one
if I did just a little less drinkin'.
Time to put somethin'
between me and the sun.
When the talkin' is over
it's time to get a gun.

Johnny (*singing*):   Caroline says she's worried,
                                 says I'm acting like a kid.
                                 She's never known anybody had a gun
                                 and her Daddy never did.
                                 But I think it should be up to me
                                 'cause when it's all said and done,
                                 somebody's got to walk into the night.
                                 Well, I'm gonna be that one.

All (*singing*):   Time to get a gun.
                             That's what I been thinkin'.
                             I could afford one
                             if I did just a little less drinkin'
                             Time to put somethin'
                             between me and the sun.
                             When the talkin' is over
                             it's time to get a gun.
                             When the talkin' is over
                             it's time to get a gun.

Johnny (*singing*):   When the talkin' is over
                                 it's time to get a gun.

END OF ACT ONE

Act two

MUSIC: "YELLOW BARLEY STRAW"

Johnny takes the unopened envelope and turns it over a few times in his hand.

All (*singing*): He's got a heart made of yellow barley straw
all wrapped up in calico patches,
and plum-chuck full of love.
He looks out over the fields
every year's losses, every year's yields,
every year's dreams, a hundred bushels
to an acre...

Johnny stands and looks out at the field. He puts the letter away in his pocket, unopened.

His heart is made of yellow barley straw...

Lights: It's a bright summer day, with not a cloud in the sky. But the tension on the ground is icy. Johnny comes out of his front stoop. McAllister stands and tries to get his attention.

McAllister: I read somewhere that the real test of a man is when he can admit that he's made a —

Johnny studiously ignores him and continues to his shop. McAllister stops mid-sentence. After a moment, a car door slams offstage and Caroline enters from the driveway with her keys in her hand. McAllister begins again.

There are lots of things in my life that I'm sorry for —

Caroline deliberately turns away and heads towards Johnny's shop.
Johnny exits with some tools in hand and nearly bumps into Caroline.
They stand awkwardly in front of each other for a moment. McAllister
interjects:

Is this how we're going to —

Johnny pushes past Caroline without speaking and heads off to Lucille
(the Mighty Big Car). Caroline throws up her arms and crosses to the
house. McAllister tries to express his sympathy.

Okay, look, all I want to say —

Caroline slams the screen door behind her, cutting him off. Johnny slams
Lucille's door shut loudly, and glares at Caroline. Caroline slams the
screen door several times in rapid succession. They glare at each other.

Given that no one was talking to anyone else, it was an oddly
noisy week.

Caroline: Mike wants to buy the farm. He told me he talked to you
last week. Were you ever going tell me? Or was it like the bills
in the basement, something you just hoped would go away?

Pause.

Are you going to say anything? Anything at all?

MUSIC: "ORDINARY GUY"

Johnny (*singing*):   I could understand if he had money.

Caroline (*speaking*): He does have money.

Johnny (*singing*):   I could understand if he had a nice car.

Caroline (*speaking*): Actually, his car is really nice. . .

Johnny (*singing*):   I could understand if he was funny,
I could understand if he was some sort of
     movie star.
But he's just a plain old ordinary guy,
with a plain old shirt and a plain old tie.

I don't know who you thought he'd be,
but he won't fight or even disagree,
and he doesn't even look a little bit like me.

Caroline (*speaking*):	**Johnny** (*singing*):
You're not even listening.	If this was what you wanted
Are you?	Why didn't you just say so?
Are you?	He's everything that I'm not
Okay, fine.	And you don't even know.

Johnny & Caroline (*singing*): He's just a plain old ordinary guy,
with a plain old shirt and a plain old tie.
I don't know who you thought he'd be,
but he won't fight or even disagree,

Johnny (*singing*):   and he doesn't even look a little bit like

Caroline (*singing*):   not a tiny bit like

Johnny (*singing*):   he doesn't even look a bit like me.

Caroline: Maybe we *should* sell, then.

Johnny: Is that what you want?

A car pulls into the driveway. Johnny squints to see who it is.
Mike enters. He nods at everyone in greeting.

Mike: Good morning, John. Mr. McAllister.

Mike extends his hand to Caroline.

> And it's Caroline, right? I'm Michael Schmidt.

McAllister: Oh, give it up.

Mike: I beg your pardon, sir?

Caroline: He saw us the other night.

Mike: Johnny. . . you can see how an innocent drink between two friends might be misinterpreted by a nosy son of —

Caroline: There's no use pretending. I told Johnny what happened.

Mike: What the heck did you do that for?

Caroline: 'Cause he's my husband.

Mike (*to Johnny*): We just had a drink, and a couple of turns on the dance floor.

Caroline: Stop it, Mike.

Mike: Look, Johnny, I —

Johnny glares at him.

Sure, I'm not the most welcome face — I don't see why all this
has to stand in the way of a good business deal.

McAllister scoffs.

McAllister: What you're doing isn't right.

Mike: Now, just a second. I left the ministry six months ago. My
exclusion period is over. It's perfectly legal.

McAllister: There's difference between what's legal and what's right.

Mike (*to Johnny and Caroline*): This is a good deal I'm offering. A chance
to get out from under. Pay those bills. I've got all the paper-
work right here.

Pause.

Caroline: There's a funny thing about the Wheat Board that I've never
figured out. Maybe you can explain it to me. Farmers can sell
wheat to them at $6.50 a bushel. And then the Wheat Board
waits until the middle of winter when people in India or China
or Europe or wherever are real hungry. Then the Board sells
it for $8.50 a bushel. What I could never figure out is. . . why
don't we didn't hold onto the wheat and sell it ourselves?

Mike: So you're saying I'm like the Wheat Marketing Board?

Caroline: I'm saying maybe we should hang onto the farm ourselves
until the highway comes along.

Mike: Are you willing to wait that long? A lot can happen between
now and then. There might be a recession. This neighbour
of yours might get that petition together. Bills might add up.
The only sure thing at this moment is. . . there's money on the
table right now.

Silence, while everyone considers things.

MUSIC: "I WANNA BUY YOUR TRUCK"

Johnny begins to sing, almost under his breath.

Johnny (*singing*):   I wanna buy your truck
I don't like what I'm doin'
I wanna give it up
I wanna try something else
I like the way that it shines

Johnny & Caroline (*singing*): Hey, I'm really stuck
In this life of mine
I wanna buy your truck

Johnny: With that lower field underwater, that's half the harvest gone.

McAllister: Johnny... Caroline... Please...

Caroline: Maybe the bank will loan us the money to plant that field again.

Johnny: I went in last week. We're up to the hilt.

Mike: You'll get a better offer from me then you will from any bank.

Johnny: This farm is done, Caroline.

Caroline: And we're not far behind. Is that what you're saying?

Johnny: I think you've made that real clear lately.

Pause. Johnny turns to Mike.

I'm not gonna shake your hand, 'cause if I get that close to you, I might punch your lights out. But you got a deal.

Mike takes a contract out of his file folder and hands it to Johnny
while McAllister narrates. Mike keeps a safe distance while he
points out where to sign.

McAllister can only shake his head ruefully at his neighbour's decision,
and bemoan what has befallen his beloved town. He turns to the audience.

MUSIC: "WHITE ROSE" (REPRISE)

McAllister (*singing*): And the girls would spend a couple of bucks,
just to meet the boys working at the pumps,
They'd grow up and fall in love
and they all moved away.
Strangers used to stop and ask
how far they'd driven off the map.
But then they built that overpass
and now they stay out on the highway.

McAllister & Caroline (*singing*): And now there's plywood for glass
where the windows all got smashed.
And there's just a chunk of concrete
where those old pumps used to stand.
There's a couple of cars half out of the ground,
and that oil sign still spins 'round and 'round,
but I guess the White Rose filling station's
just a memory now...
but I guess the White Rose filling station's
just a memory now...

McAllister: I bet by this point you're wondering why do I care so
much? No more neighbours practically in my front lawn. I can
sell too. Soon, there'll be a Walmart right where I'm standing
and I'll be a rich man. I should be dancing for joy. It broke my
heart to see my brother lose that farm thirty years ago. And
then, when Hendrik's turn came...

Another wide turn around the headland and back we go thirteen years.

Oh, bollocks. I know that look. Why you people need everything spoon-fed to you in chronological order is beyond me. There is such a thing as an emotional arc to a story, y'know. Try to steer clear of the fenceposts this time...

MUSIC: "MCALLISTER'S THEME" TAKES US INTO AND UNDERSCORES A FLASHBACK.

Lights up on Hendrik and Johnny working on the antique tractor. Hendrik is whistling "John Deere B" while he works.

McAllister: Even though they had a newer model, Hendrik and Johnny kept that old tractor running. And they never tired of showing it off.

Hendrik: She is de "John Deere B Long Frame." Met en big battery. First tractor met en electric starter. Ever.

Johnny: Not that the starter has ever worked.

Hendrik: Starter underneath tractor, behind crank. Stupid. Every time she stalls I must my head under frame put. By one hand jiggling...

He grunts as he gets into position.

...met odder hand pedal pushing.

McAllister: That tractor killed him.

Johnny exits. Hendrik busies himself hooking up the cultivator to the old tractor.

Hendrik's cows got through that fence again. On my way off to the paper I let him know. He was in the middle of cultivating the field, with the old John Deere.

Nobody will ever know what exactly happened, even though I've puzzled over it a hundred times... Maybe it stalled like it always did... maybe he got it running and then he heard a funny rattle, and leaned forward while it was moving... but Hendrik went under the wheels and got caught in that cultivator...

Hendrik loses his balance. He is trapped under the dashboard. The sound of the tractor continues as Hendrik's arm thrashes, then goes still.

I always put the weekend paper to bed on Thursdays. It was well past dark when I got back. The tractor wasn't in the drive shed. I knew that wasn't good.

McAllister finds Hendrik lying in the open field.

The cultivator had dragged him a good forty or fifty feet before it finally left him bleeding in the stubble. He was barely conscious when I found him, but by the time they loaded him in the ambulance... The doctors put enough blood in him to fill a man up three times over. But it just kept comin' outta all them holes.

A cultivator's a damned thing.

MUSIC: UNDERSCORING ENDS.

Caroline sits down beside Johnny. She's come to help him to write the eulogy. Johnny has a pad of paper and pencil in his hand. They sit in silence.

Johnny: Thanks for comin' over. I'm not doin' real well with this eulogy.

Caroline: Why don't you just say how you feel?

Johnny: I don't know how I feel, really.

Caroline: How come you never know how you feel?

Johnny: Lay off, Caroline.

Caroline: Seriously, how —

Johnny: No, seriously. Lay off.

Pause.

Caroline, now that Dad's gone, I'm gonna be takin' over the farm and the small motor business too. The only thing is. . . that house is awful big for one person.

Caroline: What're you asking?

Johnny: I'm asking you to marry me, Caroline.

Caroline: Just like that?

Johnny: Oh, sorry.

Johnny gets down on one knee.

Caroline, will you marry me?

Caroline: No, I mean — "the house is awful big for one person, so will you help me fill it out a bit." Asking someone to marry you isn't just about looking for a roommate. I need to know you're going to be there.

Johnny: I live here.

Caroline: I mean — Look, you have to promise me that once a week you'll talk about one feeling.

Johnny: What, like, every Friday at five or something?

Caroline: Yes. It's your new job. And you're gonna hate every minute of it, but you're gonna have to promise.

Johnny: Oh man. . . Okay. Deal.

Caroline: All right then, get started. What was your favourite time with your father?

Johnny: When he'd shut up.

MUSIC: "SMALL MOTORS"

Johnny (*singing*):   We'd bang on this and bang on that.
He'd adjust the timing.
Turn a mag and set the screw,
then he'd fix the idle.
Finally, he'd make them run,
as good as they were gonna be.
And everything he knew, y'know,
he taught it all to me.

And he liked small motors,
flywheels on the side,
single piston engines,
made out of cast iron.
He liked small motors.
We'd start 'em one by one.
We'd stand around and we'd listen
to them little engines run.

Lights. McAllister reveals a small headstone. We need not recreate an entire graveyard, not even a hole in the ground: as with everything else in this play, a hint of a gravestone will suffice to draw the entire scene.

McAllister: I went to the funeral, of course. Caroline looked nice. I thought Johnny was gonna choke himself with that tie.

Johnny and the rest of the cast haul several items all powered by small motors onstage: a lawnmower, a generator, a leaf blower, a water pump, an unidentifiable, nondescript motor attached to a hunk of plywood. They set them around the grave.

When we got to the gravesite, Johnny had surrounded the grave with half a dozen small motors. There were half a dozen more in the back of a pickup.

Johnny, looking uncomfortable in a suit, stands to give the eulogy. He clears his throat.

Johnny (*singing*):   Boys, I know you're in your suits
and you've come to say goodbye.
I can tell you miss him too
by the tears in your eyes.

But I'm askin' you a favour
from a boy who's broken-hearted.
Help me get these suckers down,
help me get them started.

All (*singing*):   'Cause he liked small motors,
flywheels on the side,
single piston engines
made out of cast iron.
He liked small motors.
We'd start 'em one by one.
We'd stand around and we'd listen
to them little engines run.

Johnny (*singing*):   We'd stand around and we'd listen
to them little engines

All (*singing*):   run.

*They start the various engines all at once. Some are high-pitched
altos, some are deep-toned basses, others rich and silky baritones.
Together they sound as heavenly as an agnostic choir. The sound fades.
Johnny says a silent goodbye to Hendrik. Johnny has teared up.
He tries to wipe the tears away but Caroline grabs his hands.
Johnny laughs in embarrassment, trying to make light of his feelings.*

Caroline: I'd be proud to be your wife.

Caroline kisses his mouth gently.

McAllister: I'm the one that bought that tractor for Hendrik and
Johnny. So with his father gone, I've taken it on myself to
keep an eye on Johnny for thirteen years. And I'm not about
to stop now.

MUSIC: "YELLOW BARLEY STRAW" (REPRISE).

The song returns us to the present, and ends the flashback.

All (*singing*):   Every year's losses, every year's yields.
Every year's dreams, a hundred bushels
to an acre.

*Johnny takes the unopened envelope and turns it over a few times
in his hand.*

And tomorrow, y'know,
the bank is gonna come and take it,
take it all away.
He got a letter in the mail it was only,
why it was only yesterday.
But he just goes on believing —

Caroline comes out of the house with a suitcase in her hand.

Caroline: I'm going to stay with Janet for a while. When the sale is finalized, maybe then I'll think about a place of my own.

Pause.

Aren't you going to say anything?

Johnny: Leave your keys in the mailbox when you go.

Caroline exits. Johnny pours himself a glass of whiskey. There is a long silence. Days pass. A nondescript man, a collector of antiques, politely knocks on the door of the garage.

Collector: I saw your ad on the Kijiji.

Johnny: Uh-huh.

Collector: Is that it there?

The Collector waves at the corner of the shed. At first it's not clear what he's pointing at or wants to buy. Johnny nods.

I know an agricultural museum that'll take it. They're doing a whole display on how they used to live in the old days. Original threshers, cream separators, that kind of thing. But they'll never take it at the price you're asking.

Johnny: I know what I got. Seven thousand dollars.

Collector: We're not on the Antiques Roadshow here.

Johnny: I did my research. That's the asking price on the internet.

Collector: Well, asking is one thing. Getting's another entirely.

Pause.

Johnny: I need five thousand for seed, fertilizer and fuel.

Collector: Seed? How you gonna plant seed if I buy your tractor?

Johnny: I got a '78 Massey out back. My father was a helluva mechanic. We worked on that John Deere every day.

Collector: How's the starter?

Johnny: Sometimes you gotta jiggle the contacts a little.

Collector: Five thousand, huh?

Johnny nods.

   All right.

The Collector writes out a cheque for Johnny. While he does, Johnny imagines what he'd tell his father.

MUSIC: "OLD JOHN DEERE"

Johnny (*singing*): This letter that I write to you Dad,
I will not sign my name.
Though I did not want to tell you,
I felt I had to anyway.
It's rained for weeks and it flooded the creek,
and I lost the whole crop of grain.
And the man at the bank won't loan me the money
to plant that field again.
So today, Dad, I sold the old John Deere.

The man who bought it's gonna fix it up
and put it in a museum.
Well, I guess that's where this whole thing's gone:
a picture for people to pay to look upon,
"That's how they lived in the old days son."
The sheep's in the meadow,
can't find the cows,
Little Boy Blue's got a job in town. . .

Yesterday Old McAllister came by
and I said I've had enough.
Between the government and the subsidies,
well, I just can't keep up.
And if welfare cheques was farmin',
well, I said I'd just rather not.
And he didn't say nuthin', Dad,
as I watched him drive off.
But today, Dad, I sold the old John Deere.

The man who bought it's gonna fix it up,
and put it in a museum.
Well, I guess that's where this whole thing's gone:
a picture for people to pay to look upon,
"That's how they lived in the old days, son."
The sheep's in the meadow,
can't find the cows,
Little Boy Blue's got a job in town. . .

The ghost of Hendrik appears in Johnny's imagination while the music underscores.

Hendrik: Always stay straight and true, and dings will work out. You'll see.

Johnny (*singing*):   I hope this letter finds you well,
I'm sorry how it just goes on.
But I had to tell somebody, Dad,
and you were the only one.

All (*singing*):   And today, Dad, I sold the old John Deere.

Johnny catches McAllister spying over the fence. McAllister has seen him sell the old tractor. They glare at one another.

McAllister: I can't get a fix on you, son. One minute you're ready to give up, the next you're selling your most prized possession so you can replant a field that ain't even yours anymore.

Johnny: Mind your own business, old man.

McAllister: If logic played a part in farming, then we'd all starve to death within a month. But a farmer farms the farm because he is a farmer. That's who he is and that's what he does.

Johnny: Everybody else is too polite to say it, so I'll do the favour. You're a nosy son of a bitch. Mind your own business.

Johnny stalks off. McAllister absorbs these thoughts for a moment. He shouts after Johnny.

McAllister: Maybe I will. Maybe I'll even build a twenty-foot-high fence right here, so I won't have to see you ruin your life.

Johnny: Good!

McAllister: But it won't make me wrong. A man doesn't plant a field of corn unless he's thinking of the future. A future with his wife in it.

Johnny slams the door. Lights remind us that McAllister is the narrator and that time passes at his whim.

It's funny how long you can ignore someone when you put your mind to it, even in a town this size. I went five weeks. Johnny got his seed in. But the wettest June on record turned into the driest July in decades. And Johnny was right back where he started.

The twangy strains of a country band in a bar begin and transport us into the local watering hole.

And through it all I didn't say a word. Until the eighteenth birthday party for my summer intern, from the community college. Good with a camera, but couldn't spell worth crap.

The Legion. Caroline sits on a stool at the bar.

You'll never guess who was at the bar.

McAllister freezes. Caroline hasn't seen him yet, and he waffles between sneaking away and going up to say something. He takes two steps away, thinks better of it and returns, then contemplates sneaking away again. Finally Caroline makes the decision for him.

Caroline: I can see you, Busybody.

McAllister: I wasn't sure if a hello from me would be welcomed.

Caroline: Maybe if you stick with hello and don't ask any questions. Busybody.

McAllister: Why are you calling me Busybody?

Caroline cocks an eyebrow.

That's a question, isn't it?

Caroline: So's that.

McAllister: Oh for Pete's sake, fine, have it your way.

McAllister stands and grabs his drink. On the other side of the stage Mike enters and starts to surreptitiously walk over.

Caroline: Sit down, Mac.

McAllister: I don't generally like being punished, no mater how much fun it is for —

Caroline: I said sit down!

Caroline grabs McAllister by the shirt collar and forces him to sit in the stool beside her, just as Mike sidles up to the bar.

Mike: Hi there, Caroline.

Caroline: I'm having a drink with my neighbour.

Mike: Well, I'll just sit here and mind my own business until you're done.

Caroline: You're making me uncomfortable, Mike.

Mike takes this entirely the wrong way and leans in lecherously.

Mike: Is that right? Why exactly am I makin' you uncomfortable?

Caroline (*rolling her eyes*): It was a one night stand. Five weeks ago. You were just there.

Mike: And maybe I can be there again when you've got an itch you need to scratch.

Caroline: I don't know how you got it into your head that I give a flying — anything — about you, but I don't.

Mike grabs her wrist.

Mike: That's just what you said in high school. But you sang a different tune in my truck.

Caroline: Mike, don't —

MUSIC: "FREIGHT TRAIN"

Mike (*singing*):   Well I just come down from Ottawa,
I have a great big wagon with a million dollars,
I was thinkin' about the girl I'd lost those
     years before.
I hadn't seen you for some time,
I thought that I might go on by,
when your memory came floodin' in,
and you closed that door.

Wish I was a freight train baby.
Wish I was a diesel locomotive.
I'd come whistlin' down your track,
crashin' in your door.
Wish I was a freight train baby.
Wish I didn't have a heart.
And you'd need a shovel full of coal
just to get me started.
Wish I was a freight train baby.
Wish I was a freight train. . .

Well, every time I talk to you
and I hear your jealous lies,
I feel like I've been left abandoned
on some old railway side.
And every time I hear your voice
my water just gets cold,
my stoker will not stoke,
and my boiler will not boil.

Wish I was a freight train baby.
Wish I was a diesel locomotive.
I'd come whistlin' down your track,
crashin' in your door.
Wish I was a freight train baby.
Wish I didn't have a heart.
And you'd need a shovel full of coal
just to get me started.
Wish I was a freight train baby.
Wish I was a freight train. . .

Well, every time I fell behind
and I could not get ahead,
I wish someone would pull the lever
and give me a little sand.
And every time I slip behind
even further back,
I wish some switchman would come out of the fog
and change my track.

Wish I was a freight train baby.
Wish I was a diesel locomotive.
I'd come whistlin' down your track,
crashin' in your door.
Wish I was a freight train baby.
Wish I didn't have a heart.
And you'd need a shovel full of coal
just to get me started.

Wish I was a freight train baby.
Wish I was a freight train . . .
Wish I was a freight train baby
Wish I was a —

McAllister shoves Mike from behind. Mike spills his drink on his shirt.
He turns around slowly, drawing himself up to his full height.

Mike: You made me spill my beer, old man.

McAllister: And I'll make you spill a lot more from your upper lip if
you're not careful. I was welterweight champion two years
in a row in the navy. I killed two Jerrys with my bare hands,
and I've been looking for a hat trick. Care to try your luck,
Schmidt?

McAllister does not exactly make an imposing figure, but Mike must be
drunk enough that he's seeing double, because he slowly thinks better of
pursuing this action.

Mike: Ah. She's not worth it.

McAllister watches him go and then sits back down on his stool.

Caroline: You were in World War Two?

McAllister: Heck no. I'd be ninety-one today if I was. I was just count-
ing on the fact he's too drunk to do the math. Look at my hands,
they're shaking.

Caroline: Barkeep! Get this man another beer.

McAllister: I think I'll need something a little stronger than that.

Caroline: Make that a whiskey. Thanks, Mac.

McAllister: I try not to be a "Busybody," but it's hard sometimes.

Caroline: You can stick your nose in that kind of business anytime you like. Cheers.

McAllister: Cheers.

They clink glasses.

Caroline: A man cheats on his wife so he can get some action. A woman cheats on her husband for many reasons, not all of them good and not all of them smart, but none of them simple.

McAllister: Here's to that.

Pause.

What are you waiting for, Caroline?

Caroline: What do you mean?

McAllister: If you really wanted to leave, you wouldn't be staying on your best friend's couch. You'd have your own apartment, maybe move to the city like you always wanted.

Caroline (*musing*): I'm waiting for him to live up to his promise. When we got married, I told him he was going to have to open up. I even gave him a schedule. Thirteen years later, I'm sick of the sound of my own voice.

McAllister: How long are you willing to wait?

A silence hangs between them during which McAllister tries with all his might not to offer another one of his opinions. Finally, he pats her hand and rises from his stool.

I couldn't stick around and see Caroline like that any longer. I'd been broken enough that week. I didn't make it more than a block and a half before I saw Johnny coming up the road without a jacket.

Lights on Johnny, in a daze. He's not so far gone that he's talking to himself, but he is clearly distracted by some internal demons, and not paying attention to the cars that are passing him.

Now keep in mind by this point it's ten o'clock at night. It's July, sure, but the nights get chilly. And here's Johnny walkin' — walkin', mind — along the side of the road. By the time I got my car turned around and came back the other way, Johnny had arrived at the field in front of Janet's house.

I thought maybe Johnny'd had a few too many. But I was standing close enough that I could tell he didn't smell of drink. I could see his eyes too. He was sleepwalking.

Caroline, returning from the bar, enters to see Johnny fall to his knees in front of a ploughed field. She stands aloof, with her arms crossed watching him and commenting. Coming from another direction, Mike enters, on his way back to his truck at the bar.

Johnny falls to his knees while he sings **"WORKED UP FIELD."**

The slashes (/) indicate where the following actor's text begins to overlap.

Johnny (*singing*):
I'm kneeling at the edge of a
worked up field
prayin' for the rain to fall.

I'm kneeling at the edge of a
worked up field
prayin' for the rain to fall.

I pray and pray and pray all day,
it don't rain at all.

McAllister (*speaking*):
He's just out there I don't even
know why, but he's kneeling in all
this turned up dirt, just losin' his
mind. He's prayin' and screamin'
for rain and people are driving by
and he's not stopping.

I'm standing at the end of
the platform
waiting for the train to come.
I'm standing at the end of
the platform
waiting for the train to come.

Caroline (*speaking*):
I have no clue what it's all about.
He was out by the train station.
I don't see what the difference is:
he's behavin' the same way,
he's screamin' and talkin'
and prayin' for things.

Mike (*speaking*):
It just can't happen. It's not
realistic. He just keeps getting
disappointed. He just keeps
tryin' and tryin'. It's like he's got
blinders on.

Man comes out of the station
said that there train don't run.

(*spoken*)
Who's that? You the conductor?
Sell me a ticket outta here.
I wanna go somewhere else.
Far away.

McAllister (*speaking*):
There's no trains through here
anymore, Johnny.

(*singing*)
I was standing at the end of
the road calling out her name

Mike (*speaking*):
He's not realistic at all.

Caroline (*speaking*):
He was yelling for me tonight.

Johnny (*singing*):
I was standing at the end of
the road calling' out her name
But the only word I heard
was the sound of my own pain.

He wants the train and then he
wants rain, now he wants me,
he just wants stuff, I don't what
he feels, but he's pretty into it,
/ he's really tryin', he's prayin',
he's screamin' and just goin' for
it, and if he ain't talking about
his feelings its pretty clear he's
feeling them.

Mike (*speaking*):
It just can't happen. It's not
realistic. / He just keeps getting
disappointed. He just keeps
tryin' and tryin'. Its like he's got
blinders on.

Johnny emits a low guttural growl,
somewhere deep in his belly.

McAllister (*speaking*):
He's kneeling in all this turned
up dirt, just losin' his mind.

Another growl, this time more of
a howl.

Caroline (*speaking*):
That can't be a bad thing,
when someone's that...
I dunno, what's the word... /
Passion.

Mike (*speaking*):
Passion's a good thing. / Passion
for rain, may not be realistic, but
it's a good thing.

*Johnny releases a shout at the top of his
voice, a yowl of pent-up rage and fear.*

McAllister (*speaking*):
Passion for trains is nice,
I don't think it'll make the
train come any faster.

Pause. Then:

(*singing*)
Feelings. I'll show you my feelings.

Caroline (*speaking*):
Passion for me too, can't say
there isn't.

(*singing*)
I'm kneeling at the edge of a
worked up field
prayin' for the rain to fall.

I'm kneeling at the edge of a
worked up field
prayin' for the rain to fall.

I pray and pray and pray all day,
it don't rain at all.

Back to the fields.
He's on, like, this conveyor belt,
or this. . . What would it be?
One of those things with the
horses that go round and round?

Just wants it to rain, wants me,
wants the rain,
goes back to wanting the rain.

(*to McAllister*)
Kneel down beside me.

McAllister:
Oh, I dunno. My knees aren't
what they used —

Johnny grabs McAllister's shirttail and
forces him to kneel down. Johnny looks
up at the sky soberly. He pauses for a
long time. Then:

RAIN! GIMME SOME FRICKIN'
RAIN! RIGHT FRICKIN' NOW!
RAIN! RAIN!!!

(*whispering to McAllister*)
Do you think that'll do it?

(*singing*)
I pray and pray and pray all day,

Caroline (*speaking*):
I guess that's your life,
you just get up in the morning,
you want and want and want
and then you sleep and then
you wake up and then you
try again.

it don't rain at all.

McAllister: That's when it really hit me. If I didn't want Johnny and Caroline to end up like my brother, I couldn't just sit and watch. I had to do something.

McAllister helps Johnny to his feet.

Caroline, Johnny's got some agreement he needs you to sign. You better come over tomorrow.

Mike stands in the shadows, listening. Neither Caroline nor McAllister notice him. Caroline nods at McAllister.

Caroline: I'll be there at ten.

Morning light dawns. Birds twitter to one another, announcing their locations to their mates, proclaiming their enthusiasm for the day they will spend together. There is a ruckus offstage, in the henhouse. Johnny enters at a clip with Mac's rifle. He sees a coyote running off in the distance, aims and shoots. He misses it.

Johnny: Yeah. You better run.

A car door slams offstage. Caroline enters.

Caroline: Hello, Mac. Johnny. Well, where is it?

Johnny: What?

Caroline: The agreement?

Johnny: What agreement?

Caroline: Mac says you need me to sign something or other.

Johnny: I got nothing for you to sign.

Pause. Caroline and Johnny slowly turn and look at McAllister. He shrugs sheepishly.

McAllister: I thought it was about time the pair of you had a talk.

Caroline: For cryin' out loud. Don't waste my time, Mac.

McAllister: Once upon a time this farm was owned by a Grumpy Dutchman. And once upon a time this Old Geezer who'd lived here all his life bought that Grumpy Dutchman a tractor that didn't work properly. And that tractor killed that Dutchman right out there in that field. Right. There. For thirteen years I have sat on this porch and stared at that spot. And for thirteen years I have kept trouble at bay for Hendrik's boy and the woman he loves. And I'm not stopping now just because you want me to. I seen one man come to a bad end on this farm. I'm too old to see another.

A car door slams offstage. Mike enters, with a thick, professional-looking folder under one arm.

Johnny: What are you doing here?

Mike: I might ask you the same thing. I was driving down the road and what am I surprised to see? A couple of trespassers still living on my farm.

Caroline: I was just leaving.

Mike: You better be, bitch.

Johnny: Don't you talk to her like that.

Mike: I'll talk any way I want, to a pair of trespassers. You've had fair warning. I'll get the sheriff if I have to.

McAllister: Hold your horses. You have to give these two notice or something, don't you?

Mike: I've given them notice. I sent a registered letter two weeks ago.

Caroline: What letter?

Johnny pulls the unopened envelope from his pocket.

Why don't you open these things when they arrive? Just 'cause you don't know what's happening, it doesn't mean it isn't happening.

Mike: And what's happening is that you're trespassing.

Johnny: Wait a minute. I just replanted the lower field.

Mike: That field is mine.

Johnny still has the rifle in his hands. He aims it at Mike.

Johnny: I said wait just a minute!

Mike: Whoa!

Caroline: Johnny!

Johnny: This is our home.

Mike: Watch where you're pointing that thing, you redneck.

Johnny: Shut up. Sit down. I said sit down.

Mike: Okay, okay.

McAllister: Johnny —

Caroline: Just calm —

Johnny: Shut up. All of you. I got a few things I want to say.

MUSIC: "YORK ROAD"

Johnny (*singing*):   Well, the rains left the day you went
and I never thought they would.
You turned away like all the rest
and I never thought you could.

Nothin' but rain for six weeks straight,
and the crops weren't any good.
I might as well start looking for food
with a rifle in the woods.

Johnny has momentarily turned his back on Mike. Mike tries to rise from his chair, but Johnny turns in that instant and aims the gun squarely at his chest. Caroline puts her hand to her mouth. Mike slowly sinks back into his chair.

All (*singing*):   So don't turn your back on me
I might have a gun.
Listen to what I have to say
and then you can carry on.

These are desperate days,
what's a man to do?
Time's got a little lien on me,
but I have no one to lean on to.

Johnny has his back to McAllister. Through the following verse, McAllister reaches very slowly for the telephone.

Johnny (*singing*):   Nineteen hundred and ninety-six
I took on this farm.
It was the year the Canadian government
put a tax on country charm.

When I told him I needed some time
he asked where my money had gone,
me livin' in a two-room shack
that I couldn't hardly keep warm.

*Johnny sees McAllister reaching for the telephone. He knocks it off
the table and onto the floor. He kicks it with his foot and it skitters
across the garage floor. He aims the rifle at McAllister.*

All (*singing*):   So don't turn your back on me
I might have a gun.
Listen to what I have to say
and then you can carry on.

These are desperate days,
what's a man to do?
Time's got a little lien on me,
but I have no one to lean on to.

When I was just a boy
my Daddy said to me:
"Always stay straight and true
and things will work out, you'll see."

Well, if my Daddy was here today
to listen to me sing my song,
I'd look him in the eye
and I'd tell him he was wrong.

*Caroline moves closer to Johnny. Johnny senses the movement out of
the corner of his eye and turns on Caroline with the rifle. But he cannot
bring himself to point the gun at her. Caroline advances closer.*

So don't turn your back on me
I might have a gun.
Listen to what I have to say
and then you can carry on.

Caroline is now standing so close that she can take the end of Johnny's wavering gun and slowly, slowly turn it aside. This is now the same tableau that we saw earlier, before McAllister rebooted the scene.

> These are desperate days,
> what's a man to do?
> Time's got a little lien on me,
> but I have no one to lean on to.

Johnny (*singing*):   Time's got a little lien on me,
but I have no one to lean on to.

Caroline: Yes you do.

Johnny: You slept with another man.

Caroline: Okay, okay, I slept with Dufus here. Can we move on now? Can we talk about what's going on with us?

Johnny: I think we just figured it out.

Caroline: That's just a symptom.

Johnny: It's not a sneeze, Caroline. It's adultery.

Caroline: You can't pay the Visa so you slip it to the bottom of the stack. You won't talk about what's going on with us, so that gets slipped to the bottom of the pile too. Come on, Johnny. Why are you so afraid to talk to me? What are you afraid of?

Johnny (*all of this coming out in one big rush of pent-up emotion*): That no one loves me! Because I'm a White Trash and I've got no education and I drink too much and my car won't start and I'm loser! Those are my feelings. You like them? 'Cause I don't. My feelings are scared and weak and I hate them. When I have to talk about my feelings I feel weak, I feel unlovable, I feel alone. I frickin' hate feeling alone. I want to protect myself, shut down, curl into a ball and disappear. Only no matter how hard I try I'm still here.

He laughs at himself as he winds down.

See. Who'd ever want to feel. . . all this junk inside. . . feels stupid being like this. . .

Slowly Johnny's raw emotion turns into a profound sorrow.

I don't want to be small anymore, Caroline. When I met you, I felt ten feet tall and as a big as a house. If there's one feeling I've ever had that mattered, it's that one. I want to feel that way again. With you.

Caroline: But that's who you are, Johnny Deere. . . You are all I've ever wanted.

Johnny: Yeah?

Caroline: Yeah.

Johnny (*laughing at himself again, relieved*): Phwew. That's a load off, isn't it?

Caroline: Sure is. Think we can let Mike go now?

Johnny: Sure. I've run out bullets from shooting at that stupid coyote anyway. Go on get out of here.

Johnny lowers the gun. McAllister gingerly takes it from him, just as he did at the close of Act One.

Mike: This doesn't change a thing. I'll see you two in court.

Johnny: Yes. You will.

Mike: Darn straight I will.

Johnny: And you'll see us in court again. And again. And again. Until you either run out of money or run out of steam. 'Cause we ain't goin' anywhere. Are we, Caroline?

Caroline: No. No we're not.

Johnny: You go ahead and take us for all we've got. Cause we ain't got nothin' to lose.

Mike: You haven't got a leg to stand on.

Johnny: No I don't. But I am one stubborn son-of-a-gun. I don't learn real fast, but I'm good at beating my head against a brick wall over and over again until it breaks in half. Just ask her.

Caroline: Oh, he really is. That's why I fell love with him.

Johnny: We're here and we're stayin'. And we ain't never givin' in.

Mike: We'll see.

McAllister feints at Mike. Mike exits: Johnny shouts after him.

Johnny: Yeah. You better run. (*Turning to Caroline*) And you. You better get your stuff moved back into that house.

They kiss. Lights.

MUSIC: "MCALLISTER'S STING"

McAllister: Farming isn't pretty. You have to clear the land, pick the rocks, rip out all the roots. You need to strip everything away, plough it up, break it down. That's how you make room for new growth. By turning the soil over so the seed can take root. That's what farming is: you need to destroy before you can grow.

Mike went back to Toronto or Ottawa or wherever he's from. He did try to take Johnny and Caroline to court. And me too, for aiding and abetting an attempted assault. We were all terrified that we'd end up in jail. I think the blind fear finally put Johnny in touch with his feelings.

Fortunately the recession hit a few months later, the province abandoned plans to build that highway, and Mike went bankrupt. I guess this is one instance where farmers were *helped* by the economy for a change.

Later that week, Johnny asked me for a favour. Though it had been a long time, I still had all the decorations in my shed. When Caroline came home from work, it was all set up.

Lights on a table and two chairs sitting in the middle of a vast cornfield, surrounded by tender corn shoots. The papier-mâché Buddhist temples descend from the ceiling again, each of them lit from within by a tiny twinkling light. McAllister shows Johnny and Caroline to their seats like a maître d' while he continues narrating.

We didn't know it at the time, but each of us was standing before a worked-up field, waiting for the rain to fall. And in the end, it did.

Thunder rumbles in the distance. The first drops of rain begin to fall on the lower field. Johnny and Caroline remain at the table, laughing like children in the rain.

MUSIC: "WILDER THAN HER" (REPRISE)

Johnny (*singing*):   Well, I'm wilder than her.
What else can I say?
But I guess that's why she fell in love with me.

Caroline (*singing*):   But I'm a house on fire,
I've got all those charms,

Johnny (*singing*):   I'm a house on fire too,
But I got four alarms.
And I'm wilder than her

Caroline (*singing*):   When he takes my hand,
and he looks me in the eye,

Johnny & Caroline (*singing*): I see something
that I've never seen in my life.

Johnny (*singing*):   She takes the fire,

(*with Caroline*): turns it down low.

Caroline (*singing*):   He takes the night,

(*with Johnny*) and makes it not so cold.

Johnny (*singing*):   She takes the distance

Caroline (*singing*):   (*with Johnny*) breaks it into miles.

Johnny (*singing*):   She makes my life

(*with Caroline*) just little less wild.

(*with Caroline*) 'Cause I'm wilder than her.

Caroline (*singing*):   (*with Johnny*) Drives me out of my mind.

Johnny (*singing*):   I guess she thought that
she was just one of a kind.

All (*singing*):   (*focus on girls*) But she's summer storm,
(*focus on boys*) I'm a hurricane.

Caroline (*singing*):   One just blows through town,

Johnny & The Boys (*singing*): one blows the town away

Johnny (*singing*):   And I'm wilder than her. . .

All (*singing*):   I'm wilder than her. . .

Johnny & Caroline (*singing*): I'm wilder than her. . .

Johnny and Caroline embrace, tender as young lovers.

THE END

BIOGRAPHIES

Ken Cameron is a multi-faceted playwright whose work fluctuates between popular and accessible plays and alternative theatre. On one end lie plays like *Harvest*, which was commissioned by the Blyth Festival and has been performed across Canada; and *My One And Only*, which was produced by Alberta Theatre Projects' playRites Festival, Workshop West in Edmonton and the Bridge Theatre Company in New York City. Both were published in *Harvest and Other Plays* (NeWest Press, 2010). Ken is currently being commissioned by the Stratford Festival to adapt the novel *Cue for Treason* by Geoffrey Trease.

On the other end of the spectrum, *How iRan: Three Plays for iPod*, is an iPod recording designed to be played as the audience moves through installations set amongst the stacks of a downtown library. With the iPod set to shuffle, there are over 10.6 million possible versions of the play. In creating the play, Ken interviewed twenty new immigrants to Canada, primarily (but not exclusively) individuals of Iranian ancestry based in Toronto and Kitchener, Ontario. Their combined stories are told by the three characters of the narrative. After writing the script in Calgary and recording the actors in Toronto, Ken returned to Kitchener and asked the interview subjects to construct the artwork. *How iRan: Three Plays for iPod* premiered at the IMPACT multicultural theatre festival in Kitchener and received its Calgary premiere at the High Performance Rodeo. The production has been featured in *Canadian Theatre Review*.

Ken co-founded Productive Obsession together with wife and co-Artistic Conspirator Rita Bozi as an independent inter-arts performance company. In the first year since its founding, its work was presented in Calgary, Banff, Iceland and Kitchener. One of Productive Obsessions' recent productions is *The Damage Is Done: A True Story* developed at the Cultch in Vancouver and the Banff Centre for the Arts. More of a TED Talk than a play, but more a play than a TED Talk, *The Damage Is Done* combines theatre, video, essay and modern dance into one event.

In 2012–13 Ken was artist-in-corporate-residence for First Calgary Financial Credit Union, where he took twenty-eight senior leaders through a series of excursions to plays and art galleries and connecting the creative experience of artists to techniques for innovation in the workplace. Also in 2012–13, Ken was Citizen Raconteur for the City of Calgary's Cultural Transformation Project, an initiative by the City Manager to author a new corporate narrative that would transform the thinking of 15,000 city employees which places the citizen at the centre of the transaction. Ken was the Artistic Director of the Magnetic North Theatre Festival for three years, from 2008–2010. Produced in partnership with the National Arts Centre in Ottawa and with a mandate to showcase Canada's outstanding touring productions, Magnetic North is produced in Ottawa in odd-numbered years, and in a different Canadian city each even-numbered year.

Ken Cameron Playography

How iRan: Three Plays for iPod (2013)

Dear Johnny Deere (2012)

Harvest (2008)

My Morocco (2007)

Dragonfly: Episode IV, Identity (with Anita Miotti and David van Belle) (2007)

My One And Only (2005)

Might As Well Live: The Words of Dorothy Parker (with Laura Parken) (2003)

Doppelganger (concept by Ken Cameron, based on a script by Simon Heath, with contributions from Bonnie Bowman, Rita Bozi, Ron Chambers, Doug Curtis, Elyne Quan and Eugene Stickland) (2001)

I Think I'm A Wolf! (with The Berserker Gang Collective) (1999)

Stop Thinking! (1999)

Martian (with The Shiny Beast Collective) (1998)

Alien Love Connection (1997)

The Climate: A Province in deKlein (with Doug Curtis and Laura Parken) (1997)

Fred Eaglesmith once wrote that he was born "in the springtime of the '57 Chevy". His arrival coincided neatly with the birth of rock 'n' roll, sounds he heard drifting across Lake Erie from American radio stations. Recalling those days, Fred notes in an interview for The Hugh's Room, one of his favourite venues, that "my Dad had an old console radio on top of the clothes dryer, and when Johnny Cash came on, he would put one hand on each side of the radio and really listen to that song. It really meant that much to him."

Born Frederick John Elgersma, one of nine children raised by a Dutch farming family in rural Southern Ontario, he began imitating his favourite music on a dime store guitar. At fifteen, his family lost their farm. Here Fred's bio becomes even more mythic: he hopped a freight train heading west and honed his craft in hobo camps and for crews of fellow forest firefighters before hitting the club, bar and coffeehouse scene.

In the years since hopping that train, his suitcase has overflowed with accolades: a Juno Award for Best Roots & Traditional Album; a number-one hit on the bluegrass charts with a cover of his "Thirty Years of Farming" recorded by James King; an acclaimed appearance on *The Late Show with David Letterman*; and, in the most authentic tribute of all, cover versions by some of the world's best-selling country musicians, from The Cowboy Junkies to Dar Williams. But most of Fred's twenty albums have been released on his own private label, cheekily titled "A Major Label".

These days Fred tours more than 180 dates a year in a school bus that has been converted to run on both gas and used cooking oil they get from restaurants and diners along the way. Fred's Travelling Steam Show sticks to its roots because "times are hard and things are tough for people, and we shouldn't be riding in buses that look like bachelor apartments," he states. As a result, "It makes me sound like the truth when I'm up there singing, because it is the truth."

Fred's website can be found at www.fredeaglesmith.com.

Fred Eaglesmith Discography

Tambourine (2013)

6 Volts (2011)

Cha Cha Cha (2010)

Tinderbox (2008)

Milly's Cafe (2006)

Dusty (2004)

The Official Bootleg Series, Vol. 2 (2004)

Balin (2003)

The Official Bootleg Series, Vol. 1 (2002)

Falling Stars and Broken Hearts (2002)

Live: Ralph's Last Show (2001)

50 Odd Dollars (1999)

Lipstick, Lies and Gasoline (1997)

Drive-In Movie (1995)

Paradise Motel (1994)

Things Is Changin' (1993)

There Ain't No Easy Road (1992)

Indiana Road (1987)

The Boy That Just Went Wrong (1983)

Fred Eaglesmith (1980)